Walking with Thomas Merton

Walking with Thomas Merton:

Discovering His Poetry, Essays, and Journals

by Robert Waldron

 Paulist Press • New York/Mahwah, N.J.

Cover design by Lynn Else

Library of Congress Cataloging-in-Publication Data

Waldron, Robert G.
    Walking with Thomas Merton : discovering his poetry, essays, and journals / by Robert Waldron.
        p.   cm.
    Includes bibliographical references and index.
    ISBN 0-8091-4058-6 (alk. paper)
    1. Merton, Thomas, 1915–1968—Criticism and interpretation. 2. Christianity and litera-ture—United States—History—20th century. 3. Christian poetry, American—History and crit-icism. I. Title.

PS3525.E7174 Z93 2001
818'.5409—dc21

                                                                                        2001040916

Published by
PAULIST PRESS
997 Macarthur Boulevard
Mahwah, New Jersey 07430

www.paulistpress.com

Printed and bound in the United States of America

Table of Contents

Acknowledgements

I wish to thank my editor Father Joseph Scott for all his editing expertise, patience, and generous encouragement in the preparation of this book. And thanks to the Massachusetts Chapter of the International Merton Society for all their support in the launching of my Merton Retreats at St. Stephen Priory in Dover, Massachusetts.

Dedication

*This book is dedicated to George F. Flynn
and his children:
George, Margaret, Dorothy, Robert, Helen,
Julia, and Mary*

Foreword by Patrick Hart, O.C.S.O.

In *Walking with Thomas Merton: Discovering His Poetry, Essays and Journals* Robert Waldron takes a long, loving look at the question of contemplation, poetry, and the spiritual life today. Through his reading journal we can follow the steps he took in preparation for a retreat he planned to conduct on Thomas Merton's poetry. Anyone who has ever attempted such an undertaking can easily identify with Waldron's apprehension and concern.

Waldron is attracted to keeping a journal, as were any number of well-known figures of the past, including Merton himself. The faithful keeping of a journal requires an honest unmasking of the self, which allows the reader to enter into another's intimate experiences.

The author has written a number of books, including two previous works on Thomas Merton. The first of these, *Thomas Merton in Search of His Soul*, takes a Jungian approach to Merton's life. A more recent book, *Poetry as Prayer: Thomas Merton*, deals with Merton's poetry and in particular those poems that lead the reader into meditation and prayer.

Waldron advises his readers to forget themselves and concentrate on the poem at hand, whether Hopkins, Blake, Dante, or Merton. It requires discipline of the senses and concentrated attention to get beneath the surface of a text and realize the various levels of meaning in a given poem. But the reward is well worth the effort.

As a young monk I kept a reading notebook of poems that struck me as I read them in such a way that they bordered on prayer or easily led to prayer. I find in this volume by Waldron some of the same poets, such as Traherne, Herbert, Donne, Hopkins, and Merton. Reading such poems quietly in a solitary place deepens the experience. This is what Waldron has done in this new volume in which poetry is used as a springboard to contemplation.

I was especially fascinated by Waldron's prologue, "Teaching and Contemplation," which generated such a positive response when it first appeared as an essay in the *Boston Globe*. It is an excellent introduction to Waldron and his contemplative vision. Here he refers to his thirty-one years of teaching secondary school students and his reading along with them the best literature from around the world, the classics from the past as well as more contemporary writers.

Waldron has read and studied Merton's voluminous writings over the years, but in preparing to conduct a retreat on Merton's poetry he had the leisure of a summer vacation to ponder more deeply the obscure passages of Merton the poet and to discover even more profound meanings. To do this, he followed Simone Weil's wise counsel, "Love's first step is attention." In the face of so much addiction to television, computers with video games, and just plain entertainment, Waldron rightly insists on the reader's hushed awareness. Inspired by Weil, he prays for all of us in these moving lines:

Lord,
    Teach me to be attentive
    To all your vestiges:
    To the first light,
    To the waking bird,
    To the leaf's rustle and the rain's drop,
    To the scent of water and the sky's hue
        and the rise of the wind;
Lord,
    Teach me to be so attentive that
    I shall hear the first flakes of the snow's fall.

A contemplative reading of Robert Waldron's present offering will produce fruits beyond all expectations, not the least of which will be a more complete understanding of Thomas Merton and his religious poetry, so often neglected in the past by other Merton commentators. Whereas Merton the young monk found a conflict between poetry and contemplation, the more mature monk saw the relationship of the two in a more holistic and positive way. The acid test is whether poetry—and all the arts, for that matter—lead us to the love of God and neighbor. Waldron is a follower of the later Merton and in this we can all rejoice.

Prologue:
Teaching and Contemplation[1]

It's now mid-summer. Two months ago my three classes of Boston Latin seniors graduated. They are probably now anxious about going off to college and starting a whole new life—in just a few weeks! I gave them my best efforts, and I hope it helps them to face their academic challenges. But more important, I hope I've taught them something about life, about the beauty of literature, and about the beauty of contemplation.

When I became a teacher of English thirty-one years ago, I did not realize that my educational goal would be to transform my students into contemplatives. When I use the term *contemplative* it disconcerts some public school people because of its religious connotation. My students associated contemplatives with ascetic hermits lost in mystic swoons somewhere in the desert. So let me briefly define what I mean by a contemplative: A contemplative is a person who is willing to forget the self in order to offer attention to the other.

Every day in class I ask my students to lose themselves in literary exegesis; thus, we read and analyze the best literature from around the world: Sophocles, Chaucer, Shakespeare, Keats, Tennyson, Turgenev, Chekhov, Eliot, Joyce, Hemingway,

Faulkner, Borges, Dickinson, Morrison, and many others. If I had to briefly describe my teaching methodology, I would say it is founded on attention to "the beautiful, bare text," a phrase attributed to Robert Frost.

What still surprises me is the difficulty today's students have in doing what is essentially a simple thing: paying attention. They're accustomed to allowing their minds to wander off in a multitude of directions. At the press of a finger, they command countless television channels, computers with video games and search engines, and MTV with its myriad images. So much entertainment at their beck and call, all instantaneous.

Consequently, educators today aren't surprised by the number of students plagued by attention deficit disorders or by those who find it arduous to focus their attention on a line of poetry or a metaphor or an algebra problem. When students are inattentive in my class, I ask them to forget themselves for a forty-minute period. I suggest they place their worries, preoccupations, and daydreams on the back burner of their minds, along with their plans for the weekend. I encourage them to devote their attention to the text in question.

I ask them, in other words, to be contemplatives!

The best explanation of what I try to accomplish is illustrated by the opening of Hemingway's beautiful short story "Big Two-Hearted River." Nick Adams has just disembarked from the train at the devastated town of Seney. He is a young man hurt in body, mind, and soul. He comes to the bridge over the Black River. He looks down into the clear water and sees some trout. ("Nick watched them a long time."[2]) He watches so long and so intently that eventually he notices the big trout at the bottom, holding themselves at the river's bed gravel. He finds them very "satisfactory." By long, intense gazing, Nick sees something he had never seen before: where the big trout hide themselves.

I have students read the text closely, whether it's a poem, novel, play, or short story. I urge them not to be satisfied with the surface meanings of plot, character and setting, and all that is obvious. My daily mantra to them is "Go deeper." Even when we have penetrated deeply into a text, I'll find myself saying, "Can we go still deeper?" Oftentimes we do, discovering the big "trout" of meaning that lies far beneath the surface.

To find literature's deeper meanings, students must forget themselves for a little while, taking the plunge into what the French call *explication de texte*. Later, they invariably confess how enriching it was to have probed at greater depth; they admit that the exegesis was worth the effort because it uncovered meanings they had been blind to.

Their acute attention achieves more than an understanding of a text, however. Besides comprehending some of the world's greatest literature, they become people who can give their attention to the world, nature, friends, relatives, strangers, and those who suffer. In their practice of attention, they see things from another's perspective, not just their own; they experience the joy of self-forgetting. In short, they've prepared themselves to become sensitive human beings capable of compassion and even of love. Like Simone Weil, I have come to believe that love's first step is attention.

Something as simple as reading a poem thus becomes a rather profound classroom activity. For instance, when my students and I study a poem, we create an ambiance necessary for a successful class. Silence must be established. We all then listen carefully as one student reads the poem aloud. Afterward, we read the poem orally in unison. Then we begin our discussion. Our attention shifts back and forth between text and the students' questions, speculations, and insights. Their remarks delve more deeply; they scrutinize the text and begin to pierce the surface of the text's "water." Altruism is fostered because the students help one another to see; in effect, they learn to see through the eyes of their peers. Thus, the class endeavor becomes a collective lesson in contemplation! And what I relish most is the possibility for any of us to experience an epiphany, one with the potential to transform our lives. As critic and philosopher George Steiner says in his autobiographical *Errata*, literature possesses the power to "transmute us."[3]

All of this I find rewarding. But there is another reward, one that lies in the future. Someday, when one of my students finds herself attentively appreciating a flower's blossom or a Rothko painting or a Mozart sonata or an obscure poem or the smile of an elderly grandparent, I may have in my small way contributed to that moment.

And that is satisfactory!

Introduction

I have always been drawn to journals, perhaps because the journal format invites spontaneity and honesty. Thus, journal writers present themselves unmasked, and the reader experiences an intimacy not felt in other literary genres. Some of the great journals of our time are those of Andre Gide, Virginia Woolfe, Raissa Maritain, Pope John XXIII, Julian Green, Henri Nouwen and, of course, Thomas Merton.

As a young man I remember being engrossed by Merton's first published journal, *The Sign of Jonas*, which for many years remained my favorite Merton book. I was intrigued by its inside peek at the Abbey of Our Lady of Gethsemani and the intimate details of a monk's life. Certainly my youthful romanticism drew me to this book, but I was also inspired by Merton's recorded efforts to be a holy man. Merton was imbued with the idea that the goal of every Catholic is to be a saint. Even after his entry into the monastery, Merton never ceased from his journal-keeping, faithfully chronicling his search for holiness within the walls of the Abbey of Gethsemani.

Now all seven volumes of Merton's unexpurgated journals have been published by HarperSanFrancisco. For those who are daunted by the sheer volume of his journals, there is now available Patrick Hart and Jonathan Montaldo's *The Intimate Merton,* a diary-like memoir composed of Merton's most poignant and insightful journal entries culled from the seven journals, covering twenty-nine years of Merton's life. This particular book inspired me to resume keeping a journal.

When I was a teenager I kept a journal, a practice I began shortly after reading *The Sign of Jonas.* I believed it would help me grow spiritually and intellectually, teach me to focus on what is important, and, I hoped, help me move toward greater self-knowledge. From the very beginning of my inner journey, Merton has served as my spiritual mentor. Now in my fifties I look back and consider myself fortunate to have met Merton so early in my life. I can confidently state that no other essayist, diarist, poet, letter writer, or novelist (Merton is all of these!) has ever exerted a greater influence on my life than the Trappist from Kentucky. From my first readings of Merton, I felt I was gazing into my own soul.

This year I decided that I would offer a Merton retreat. Lecturing on Merton's life had become second nature for me ever since I published my first book on Merton in 1994, *Thomas Merton in Search of His Soul.* Then in June 2000, I published *Poetry as Prayer: Thomas Merton.* My second book focuses on Merton's poetry. I had always wanted to give poetry retreats because I believe in the affinity between poetry and prayer and poetry's power to lead attentive readers into a deeper spiritual life. So I decided to combine my two great loves, Merton and poetry, by offering a Merton poetry retreat at St. Stephen Priory in Dover, Massachusetts.

In preparation for my retreat I reread as much of Merton as I could in a summer's time. I also kept a journal of my journey through his writing, recording spontaneously my reactions, thoughts, insights, and questions. It was an exhilarating experience; it was, in fact, like reading Merton for the first time. My summer's reading, to my delight, yielded a new appreciation for Merton the man, the monk, the priest, and finally for Merton the poet.

I can now say that Merton is no longer my mentor; he is, rather, my friend. I know him better than any other author because Merton is the most unmasked writer I've ever encountered. He held nothing back from his journals; he stands before us "naked."

Merton's utter truthfulness likely disconcerted a few of his readers. For instance, Merton is totally honest about his love affair with his nurse, M. He didn't have to record its course from beginning to end, so why did he? To show us, I believe, what it means to be human. Yes, Merton is a writer for all seasons and for all men and women. He is so very human and flawed, and because of this he offers us all perennial hope.

I hope that as you join me in my journal-walk with Merton, you too will get to know him, to allow him to be a friend. Perhaps in Merton you'll find the saving words to assist you on your journey to holiness/wholeness. That is my intent and my prayer.

Preparing for the Retreat

This year's teaching is finished! Here I am in my quiet study with windows overlooking my neat lawn. The maple tree is in full leaf, the sky blue, the weather warm but comfortable. I have now before me a summer of no pressing obligations. A time for spiritual renewal. A time to prepare myself for my first day-long Merton retreat to be given on September 23 at the Dominican Priory in Dover, Massachusetts. A summer with Merton will be exactly what I need to prepare myself.

After thirty-one years of teaching, I have decided to retire within two years and pursue my dream: writing books and directing poetry retreats.

I've always longed to direct poetry retreats, but I'm a bit nervous about it. I'll ready myself by devoting my summer days to rereading Merton, thinking about him, and meditating upon his work.

Such a summer will be time well spent, both for the mind and soul.

I'll tackle his complete poetic opus. I'll plumb my own reasons for my fascination with Merton. I'll examine why I've chosen him as my mentor. Indeed, was it a matter of choice?

Why does the word *contemplative* bring a smile to my lips?

As a teenager in the 1960s, I was (and remain) intrigued by contemplation and its invitation to a deeper life in God. In my junior year of high school, I discovered *The Seven Storey Mountain*. I became enthralled with monastic life. And with contemplation. After reading Merton, I decided I too wanted to be a contemplative with its promise of experiencing God. What greater goal could there be in life?

Merton will be my daily summer companion. A trip to Europe would be fun, but I have an obligation to my September retreatants: I must know my subject as thoroughly as I can. Even though I've devoted the last twenty years to reading Merton, and written two books about him, I still have not read all of his books. Yes, there's more work to do.

An offer from a friend to travel to England. But I refuse.

"Another book on Merton?" she says, arching her brow.

"Yes, another one," I say, proudly.

"But why?"

"Because I'm hooked on Merton," I say, smiling.

"Well, if you have to be addicted to something, Merton's okay. But I still don't get it."

"When will you read Merton?" I say for the thousandth time.

She now smiles, "Sometimes it's better to save the best for last...but I will someday."

I smile and nod and wonder how she knows Merton's "the best."

I grow more anxious about my retreat. Of course, jitters are to be expected. To go from teacher to retreat director is a huge leap. But in many ways the preparation is similar. I must steep myself in the work, become one with it so that when I stand before people, I'll not have to refer to lecture notes.

I must let Merton seep not only into my mind but also into my soul.

I mustn't turn my retreat into an ego trip. As a teacher I've had to adopt the useful personae of actor and entertainer to keep my students' attention. I sometimes can be quite the ham in displaying my bag of tricks. My retreat goal isn't to entertain—though now and again I may relate an amusing anecdote—but to point my finger toward Merton and to lead them toward a deeper understanding of his life and in particular his verse, which is, for many Merton aficionados, the most unexplored portion of Merton's opus.

His verse speaks eloquently to us about all aspects of his life. Our reading of his poetry, I hope, will also become our prayer.

When I wrote my book on Francis Thompson's poem "The Hound of Heaven," my publisher liked the idea of "praying poetry." I had discovered, in my study of Thompson's great ode, that I entered a domain beyond explication, one of prayer. Surely in the beginning of my work on the poem, I needed to dominate it intellectually, to understand its more obscure lines, symbols, and themes. After a while, however, I found that I had lost myself in the poem's beauty, in its holy theme: God's loving pursuit of Francis Thompson (and of Everyman). I became one with the poem. Through attention, the aesthetic experience transformed itself into one of prayer, into a marriage of the aesthetic and spiritual. Later, because it had taken on the quality of prayer, I would read the first stanza of "The Hound of Heaven" every day as if it were a psalm:

> I fled Him, down the nights and down the days;
>   I fled Him, down the arches of the years;
> I fled Him, down the labyrinthine ways
>   Of my own mind; and in the mist of tears
> I hid from Him, and under running laughter.
>   Up vistaed hopes I sped;
>   And shot, precipitated,
> Adown Titanic glooms of chasmèd fears,
> From those strong Feet that followed, followed after.
>   But with unhurrying chase,
>   And unperturbèd pace,
> Deliberate speed, majestic instancy,
>   They beat—and a Voice beat
>   More instant than the Feet—
> "All things betray thee, who betrayest Me."[4]

Poems as prayer. This is the concept my publisher has adopted for a new series of books: "Poetry as Prayer" books. Three have been published thus far: on the Hound, on Merton, and the third on the Carmelite poet Jessica Powers. Others on Hopkins, the psalms, and Denise Levertov are in the works.

I've decided on the retreat theme: *Contemplation, Poetry, and the Spiritual Life.* That is a good general title. Specifically what I aim for is the opening of the spiritual eye of attention.

I refuse to allow myself to get bogged down about whether or not Merton is a major or minor poet. Who cares! The fact of the matter is that he wrote some very fine poetry. When I read his verse and prose, I feel more alive, and if that's not the best litmus test of fine writing, then I don't know what is.

To my mind, "Night-Flowering Cactus" is one of the loveliest poems about the contemplative life I've ever read. A rich, deep poem that every lover of poetry will appreciate. And I shall include it in the packet of poems I offer my retreatants.

Bright sun, clear sky. Began the morning with classical music as I do every day. Today I chose Claudio Arrau's Beethoven concertos. B's music energizes me; Merton has a similar effect on me. Music and Merton's effect on the soul: something to explore.

I remember a brief conversation with poet and biographer Paul Mariani. As a young scholar, he searched for the distinctive Catholic voice among American poets. He thought he found it in Merton (born in France, Merton became an American citizen). He decided after further studying, however, that Merton's verse lacked greatness. Of course there is John Berryman's verse, a good candidate, and Mariani wrote a fine biography of him. Later, he wrote one of the Catholic convert Robert Lowell.

But I don't believe he ever found the one, great, singular American Catholic poetic voice. Perhaps he's still searching.

The American Catholic voice in prose? Perhaps F. Scott Fitzgerald. Embarrassed about being a Catholic, he couldn't escape its influence, particularly noticeable in *The Great Gatsby*, his masterpiece.

Perhaps there is a male or female Catholic Emily Dickinson out there, living and writing alone. And unpublished. Perhaps in a hundred years an antique dealer will discover the poet's desk and find within it a secret drawer crammed with poems of greatness.

A hundred years from now Merton will still be read, of that I've no doubt.

Today I visited the New England Mobile Book Fair, best place in the Boston area for marked-down books. The ascetic face on a book's cover drew me: it was an angular, El Greco-like visage of a man sitting on the ground with a dark sky behind him. On closer look I saw that it was Robert Lax, Merton's old buddy from his Columbia University days. I couldn't resist the impulse to purchase *Love Had a Compass: Journals and Poetry of Robert Lax.*

It was Lax who reminded Merton, in *Seven Storey Mountain*, that to be a saint is every Catholic's goal. My friend Jonathan Montaldo once said it was probably the worst advice Lax could have offered Merton. Merton tried to be a saint in the early years of his monastic life. Gradually he realized that being himself was work enough. To be himself, he'd learn, meant knowing the True Self.

The True Self is the goal of everyone's journey.

Last night I read Lax's poem "Circus of the Sun"; it is childlike in its simplicity. Reminds me of Blake's "Songs of Innocence."

One line moved me: "Have you looked at spheres of dew on spears of grass?"[5] Such *carpe diem* delight in nature's diminutives. Reminds me of Dickinson and of course Whitman.

Lax captures the whole of Merton in his phrase "a certainty of tread." The passage reads:

July 24/69

> it must be one thing to imagine what a guru is like, another to see one. seeing merton was little enough like seeing an imaginary guru.
>
> yet he had one quality, particularly in the last years, but even (to a large degree) from always, from even before he (formally) became a catholic: a certainty of tread.
>
> that might sound as though he plonk plonk plonked like a german soldier as he walked down the street. actually, he didn't: he danced (danced almost like fred astaire: bang bang bang; or bojangles robinson, tappety bam bam bam) but he knew where he was dancing.[6]

Merton didn't always know where he was going. I have here on my desk his famous prayer; it begins, "My Lord God, I have no idea where I am going. I do not see the road ahead of me. I cannot know for certain where it will end."[7]

But not knowing his destination didn't stop him from walking, running, and dancing. He was intent upon the journey no matter where it led, and it led to many strange places, some fraught with danger. But he journeyed no matter the risk. Anyone who dismisses Merton as an escapist because he "fled" into a monastery doesn't know Merton. Or any monk for that matter. Escapists don't last long in monasteries.

But Merton never traveled alone; he brought along with him the poets who "sang" him into the church: Dante, William Blake, Gerard Manley Hopkins, T. S. Eliot, Federico Garcia Lorca, Rainer Maria Rilke, and so many others. I am always touched when I recall Merton's jumping up from reading Lahey's biography of Gerard Manley Hopkins to dash off to Corpus Christ Church to become a Catholic. That tread—rather a leap!—definitely had certainty.

Lax understands that the description of "guru" doesn't fit Merton. I too don't like the image it conjures up: an omniscient sage sitting upon a silken pillow spouting "wisdom." No, Merton knew himself too well and refused to assume the role of prophet; we see this refusal in his poem "Elias: Variations on a Theme." That didn't rule out his willingness to share with others what he learned about the spiritual journey. He was a master of sharing.

Oh, he was sometimes annoyingly preachy throughout his autobiography, and it spilled over into the first version of *Seeds of Contemplation,* but he stopped short of making a fool of himself. Nor did he want to become a Catholic apologist; he left that to experts like Fulton Sheen, whom he admired.

In this century Merton is one of the greatest cartographers of the inner journey, and for that we all can be thankful because his "markings"—Thank you, Dag Hammarskjöld—help all of us along the contemplative way.

It is now 7 A.M. I've watered the lawn and the garden and taken the dog for a walk in the clean morning air. My walk is more like meditation as I enjoy the pale blue sky and allow my mind to wander where it will. I feel no stress and decide a walk with the dog is a good way to prepare myself for today's reading and writing.

I'll divide the retreat into two sessions: the morning session (9:30–11:30 A.M.) will address Merton's biography. I'll have to start from scratch because there are bound to be people who know little about Merton. The afternoon session (1–4:00 P.M.) I'll devote to Merton's definition of contemplation and to a reading of several of his best poems. I must explain his early dualistic dilemma: seeing contemplation and poetry as mutually exclusive. Reconciliation between the two did not come easy. I must explore *how* he achieved his reconciliation.

I suspect he wouldn't face the same problem today. Pope John Paul's *Letter to Artists* clearly delineates the role of artists in the modern world. Too bad something like this letter wasn't available for the young Merton; it would have saved him much anguish.

During the retreat there must also be time for dialogue and for solitary reflection. The grounds of St. Stephen's Priory are beautiful with sweeping lawns and well-spaced trees, a perfect place for silence and meditation. I hope the retreatants will savor its quiet beauty. (When driving through St. Stephen's gate and along its tree-arched lane, does everyone think of novelist du Maurier's Manderley?) I'll set aside a twenty-minute period for reflection both in the morning and afternoon. Perhaps before Mass and after lunch.

Today I was informed that Kathleen Norris will review my books on the Hound of Heaven and Merton for *America* magazine. Hope it's a positive commentary. I'd appreciate some good publicity since my publishers don't widely advertise their books. I gather it's too expensive.

A review can make or break a book. It's unfair, but critics possess a lot of power. I think of poor May Sarton who became ill after a devastating review of her novels. Later, it happened to her good friend Doris Grumbach. Both were dumbfounded and made physically ill by the gratuitous cruelty.

I could never tear apart someone's work, no matter how bad. Anyway, I don't feel that secure in judging whether or not something is good or bad. Of course, there are the critics with axes to grind—but they shouldn't grind them on people's feelings.

Merton rarely received bad reviews. In fact, he was his own worst critic and dismissed several of his books as outright bad. In his personal hierarchy from awful to best books, he listed none under "best." I'd say he was being rather harsh on himself. But he always suffered from a streak of perfectionism.

Just when my solitude deepens, interruption rears one of its many heads. The lawn must be mowed, the shrubbery cut, the flowers watered. Then there are the phone calls and visitors. I haven't told anyone about my summer with Merton. I want my life to remain as ordinary as possible. I don't intend to become a hermit, although I go days without seeing anyone.

For the past two days I've lived with a skunk in my basement! How it managed to enter is a mystery because my suburban home is as tight as a drum. Finally, a clever man from the New England Wildlife Association managed to lure it out of a basement window. Turned out to be a baby skunk that somehow lost its mother. It left a calling card in its sprayed scent. Enough to cause a slight wrinkling of the nose.

I think of Merton and all the "little" interruptions to his silence and solitude. The guns of Fort Knox surely topped his list. The constant barrage of visitors and letters must have also taken their toll on his patience and good heart. He usually received everyone and answered most of his letters. All the price of his fame.

I can understand his desire for a hermitage, but one like his with a telephone and so near the monastery was certainly not the answer to his prayers.

I must always keep in mind that his primary goal was a deep, contemplative relationship with God. As early as *Tears of the Blind Lions,* in 1949, Merton pledged his allegiance to contemplation,

> May my bones burn and ravens eat my flesh
> If I forget thee, contemplation.[8]

I too must be loyal to my resolution. Daily I must read and write about Merton. Daily I must pray his poems. Daily I must attempt to understand why he chose the life of a Cistercian contemplative. Daily I must try to plumb the reasons for my own fascination with Merton's life and work.

Just finished reading Merton's *What Is Contemplation?*. For anyone new to Merton, it's a good place to begin because it's brief and to the point. Merton never succumbs to the esoteric; he always uses simple language. Lax recalls that in their Columbia days Merton and he promised to follow simplicity both in their speaking and writing. They succeeded.

From Merton's book I leave with several insights. When he wrote it in 1950, he was still imbued with a dualistic perspective: the "bad" world out there and us, the good contemplatives, here inside Gethsemani. But the world is not the enemy. The world is beautiful, and God can be found there too. He states that contemplation is a gift of the Holy Spirit, but suggests it's not a good idea to desire contemplation for its own sake. It's not to be a spiritual ego trip.

Lastly, Merton reminds us that all contemplation is a gift of God's love for us. I desire contemplation because I know it is right and good to predispose myself to God's grace in any fashion God wishes to grant it to me.

I also like Merton's drawings. He inherited his father's artistic talent. The face of Christ Crucified on page 75 is moving. The Christ he first began to know during his first trip to Italy when he was only a teenager. It represents the Christ of Rome's Byzantine mosaics. For Merton, all roads lead to Christ. No escaping this truth.

The best commentary on Merton's pursuit of contemplation is William Shannon's *Thomas Merton's Paradise Journey*; it is a rewrite of his earlier *Thomas Merton's Dark Path,* and masterfully done. Shannon comments at length on Merton's treatise "The Inner Experience," an unfinished work that Merton left orders not be published.

Merton was ambivalent about who could be a contemplative. On one hand, he says, all Christians have the seeds of contemplation planted within at baptism. On the other hand, he fears only a few will ever become pure contemplatives because only a few will elect to live within the silent and solitary ambience of contemplative orders. Such an idea is the fruit of the spiritual athletes syndrome.

Again, Merton was a victim of dualism, an either/or mentality, but the more he entered his own contemplative experience, the more he embraced the world. The sign of the true contemplative is love and an all-embracing acceptance. In the mystical body of Christ, no one is "better" because he's a contemplative, or "inferior" because she isn't.

If God so desires it, anyone can be a contemplative. In my home with its numerous interruptions I can be a contemplative if God so wills it. I'd wager that Merton's life overflowed with more activity than mine. And, despite this, he managed to cultivate a deep spiritual life.

Merton says that *kenosis* (emptiness) is the sine qua non of the contemplative life. An emptiness to be filled by Christ. By this he means a stripping away of self, of all that is egotistic.

Even as a sixteen-year-old prep school student, Merton loved poetry. In a very early essay he exhibits not only a flair for writing but also a talent for close reading of verse. He was pessimistic about poetry's chance to survive the twentieth century. Understandable for a young person born during World War I and living through the Great Depression. He particularly liked the "sweet melancholy" of Rupert Brooke's verse. His essay on modern poetry won the Bailey English Prize at Oakham School in 1931.

Today I picked up my icon. When I first gazed upon it, I instantly saw that the artist had captured what I had asked for: Christ's radiant compassion.

Russian artist Victor Anoufrieve is becoming well known for his icons. I saw an exhibition of his work at Boston's Franciscan Shrine. The next day I commissioned an icon. The only stipulation was that the face of Christ show his radiant compassion. It does!

Of course, my reason for wanting an icon is prayer. I'd read Merton's friend Jim Forest's book about praying with icons. I also heard Forest speak at Boston College. I was moved when at one point he quietly took an icon from his pocket, kissed it, and put it back.

Merton was also intrigued by the spiritual power of icons, these "windows upon eternity." He had several in his hermitage chapel. It's also touching to read the list of his effects after his accidental death:

    1 pair of dark glasses in tortoise frames
    2 pairs of bifocal eyeglasses in plastic frames
    2 Cistercian leather-bound breviaries

1 rosary (broken)
1 small icon on wood of Virgin and Child

I just checked with Merton's first volume of letters, *The Hidden Ground of Love.* In 1965, Sufi scholar Marco Pallis gifted Merton with an icon. Pallis wrote, "Here is a small token of my love: this ikon, Greek, probably Macedonian, of the date probably 1700...seems well-fitted to make its home in a Cistercian setting."[9]

Merton was overwhelmed. He writes, "I have never received such a precious and magnificent gift from anyone in my life."[10] A note at the end of the letter indicates that the icon now hangs in Merton's last hermitage. Last year I visited Gethsemani. I saw the hermitage and considered it a privilege, but its door was locked and I wasn't able to enter. Not to see the inside and feel its aura was a disappointment. Brother Hart saw my emotion and invited me to return to Gethsemani for a personal tour of the hermitage.

In a letter to Pallis, Merton says the icon will serve as a reminder to pray. I find myself returning to my Compassionate Christ to gaze upon it and recite the Jesus Prayer, a favorite prayer of Merton's, and to make the sign of the cross.

When Merton had been gifted with an icon, a depiction of St. Elias, he said, "What a thing to have in the room. It transfigures everything."[11]

I consider Merton's opus to be a word icon. The untold number of people brought to prayer and contemplation through Merton's writing. How many lives transfigured?

A beautiful summer day. My cousin Angus planted a plum tree on my front lawn. With my high blood pressure, I dared not do it myself. Even in his 50s Merton would have done it quickly and efficiently. He was strong with the build of a peasant. The incongruity of his physical build and his elegant mind! He looked like novelist Henry Miller. In fact, Miller and he shared the same publisher, James Laughlin's New Directions Press. Merton was briefly embarrassed by this. Later, he perceived its irony and humor.

I can easily imagine Miller and Merton talking through the night while drinking Scotch and water. Both exchanging stories of their early romantic conquests. Merton about his Augustinian days before his conversion. He was an earthy man.

Today I received an inquiry about my poetry retreats from Genesis Spiritual Life Center's Program Coordinator, Ann McGaharn. This makes me happy; it's what I hope to do in my future, to show the affinity between religious poetry and prayer.

My Merton retreat is totally focused on Merton's life and work. A full weekend retreat could also be devoted to Merton. I would, however, prefer to include other poets besides Merton: Francis Thompson, Gerard Manley Hopkins, T. S. Eliot, R. S. Thomas, Denise Levertov, and many others. But at first I think I'll stick with Merton.

When I first began to read Merton, I searched for his method of prayer, but he rarely succumbs to methodology. A wise decision on his part because so much of prayer and contemplation is of an ineffable order.

Merton lets his guard down about his personal prayer life in a letter to the Sufi Absul Aziz. Merton writes:

> Strictly speaking I have a very simple way of prayer. It is centered entirely on attention to the presence of God and to His will and His love. That is to say it is centered on faith by which alone we can know the presence of God...it is a matter of adoring Him as invisible and infinitely beyond our comprehension, and realizing Him as all...My prayer is then a kind of praise rising up out of the center of Nothing and Silence.[12]

His definition of prayer is similar to Simone Weil's idea that attention is prayer. She says that self-forgetting via attention is the doorway to contemplation.

I'm rereading *The Seven Storey Mountain*. Many Merton admirers ignore his temptation to suicide while staying at the Pennsylvania Hotel in 1936 when he was twenty-one. The scene is riveting. It was a close call for Merton; he was wise to check himself out of the hotel and to return to his grandparents' house. He felt he was on the brink of a nervous breakdown, and he likely was. At the end of the chapter, Merton describes himself as a wounded modern man. The title of Jung's *Modern Man in Search of a Soul* is such an apt description of the young Merton.

What he desired was a death to the old self and a rebirth of the new. He found rebirth within Christianity, as had T. S. Eliot in 1928. I must explore more deeply the similarities between these two poet-converts. The biggest difference is that Eliot refused to go all the way to Rome, choosing instead the Anglo-Catholic Church. Surely his own class prejudice against Catholics had something to do with his decision, as well as his rejection of the dogma of the pope's infallibility.

Catholic converts among poets: Gerard Manley Hopkins, David Jones, Siegfried Sassoon, Edith Sitwell, Kathleen Raine, Robert Lowell, Robert Lax, Denise Levertov, Annie Dillard, and Wallace Stevens.

Merton admired Eliot's verse, especially his *Four Quartets;* he described it as some of the finest verse written in the twentieth century. That and Rilke's *Duino Elegies.*

Merton regarded Francis Thompson's "The Hound of Heaven" as a good poem. Not high praise, but praise nevertheless.

I have given a goodly portion of my life to the Hound. My commentary on the ode and my novel about Thompson's life are tangible proof of my fascination with the opium addicted poet. One could say that God hounded Merton into the Catholic Church, into Gethsemani and into the priesthood and later into the hermitage. Yes, he was definitely a God-hounded man, as well as God-haunted—there's a difference—as all contemplatives know.

Merton was also hounded by his need for solitude. He considered entering the more solitary Carthusians until his confessor advised him to dismiss departure from Gethsemani as a temptation. It worked!

The finest books I ever read about solitude are poet/novelist May Sarton's *Journal of Solitude* and Merton's *Thoughts in Solitude*. Come to find out, however, that Sarton was rarely alone in either of her homes, in New Hampshire and Maine. Friends were constantly dropping in or staying with her; she also maintained as large a correspondence as Merton had.

Merton too was rarely alone, by which I mean by himself. Always surrounded by his Cistercian brothers. Always visitors to the monastery, seeking him out. Ever-arriving letters to be answered. Constant requests for books and book reviews and political and theological commentary. The man was just too busy. No wonder he prayed to become a hermit.

Sarton and Merton were both writers who craved solitude because it was the very thing they lacked. They were also two charismatic personalities who naturally drew people to them. Not a good combination.

Afternoon silence shattered by my neighbor's droning shears. For three hours he sculpted his shrubbery. Little did he know that he cut into my working hours, and my reading of Merton. Oh well, the racket at least helps me understand what Merton felt when those dreadful Fort Knox guns shattered the Kentucky quiet.

It's been a long time since I've experienced complete silence. My best silent days have been spent on retreats at St. Joseph's Abbey in Spencer, Massachusetts. On last winter's retreat, the beautiful monastic grounds were covered in a mantle of snow.

Walking to the bookstore, I marveled at the silence: no people, no cars, no planes, no bird song, no wind, and no gurgling stream, which was frozen. Utter silence. Its effect on me was an increased if not exquisite attention to my surroundings. I felt as if I was on the threshold of some revelation, a glimpse beyond the veil. But nothing happened out of the ordinary, unless one considers acute attention unusual.

In the silence I prayed for all those I love.

Spent the morning viewing the Vincent Van Gogh exhibit at the Museum of Fine Arts in Boston. Vincent's self-portraits and portraits of friends profoundly impressed me. He captures the essence of people, penetrating to their very soul. Strange, standing before lifelike faces with their eyes staring into mine. If they could talk, what would they say to me about life?

How amused Vincent would be by the prices his work now commands, he who sold only one painting during his lifetime. Vincent was a tortured soul who identified with the poor. Something definitely Christ-like about Vincent.

When I returned home, I looked at some of John Howard Griffin's photo-portraits of Merton. He too tried to capture the essence of those he photographed. I remember my high school English teacher holding up one of Griffin's most famous pictures of Merton. "Look at his Mona Lisa smile," Sister said. Then she further remarked, holding the picture higher for the whole class to see, "He knows the secret; you can see it in the twinkle of his eye."

Perhaps my own fascination with Merton commenced with Sister's small photo and her off-the-cuff remark about the secret.

Seeing the Van Gogh exhibit brings to mind Merton's father Owen Merton, an artist from New Zealand. Merton describes his father as an artist who painted like Cezanne. Jonathan Montaldo has graced the Merton Center at Bellarmine College with several Owen Merton paintings. They do indeed remind one of Cezanne. Especially in his depiction of trees. But it was a winter scene that moved me.

Like Van Gogh, Owen Merton was not a particularly successful painter. His son's fame has, I'm informed, raised the prices of his work.

Usually people begin their Merton study with his autobiography. The next book they read is often *New Seeds of Contemplation*, now considered a spiritual classic. Its format is inviting: brief passages on various aspects of the contemplative life. Brief because Merton invites the reader to reflect on his own reflections. His book isn't meant to be read in one sitting. Such a reading would nullify the purpose of the book: to create space, time, and peace for short periods of quiet contemplation.

On the flyleaf of my copy of *New Seeds* I've inscribed my name and "September, 1981, Boston." Almost two decades have passed. And in all that time I've continued to read Merton. It struck me today that if it weren't for Merton I wouldn't have begun my day praying before an icon of Christ. Like many Americans, I'd likely have been caught up in the daily pursuit of the American Dream with its concomitant pursuit of money and status—and no time for quiet prayer.

On page 1 of *New Seeds* three sentences leap up at me: "[Contemplation] is that life itself, fully awake, fully alive, fully aware that it is alive. It is spiritual wonder. It is the spontaneous awe at the sacredness of life, of being."[13]

"It is spiritual wonder." A beautiful, simple sentence. I have read something recently that echoes this declaration. I go to my library shelf and take down Pope John Paul II's *Letter to Artists*. I read on page 32: "On the threshold of the Third Millennium, my hope for all of you who are artists is that you will have an especially intense experience of creative inspiration. May the beauty which you pass on to generations still to come be such that it will *stir them to wonder!*"[14]

This has been a good week. Merton and I had a quality time together. Even the silence between passages of *New Seeds* is full. He reveals more of himself, and I sit back and take it all in. If I had ever met Merton, I know I would have been too shy to say much. Anyway, I'd rather listen to him. As I'm doing now. Although he was a connoisseur of silence and solitude, if I had dropped in on him, he would have welcomed a visitor. That's how kind he was.

It's been thirty-two years since Merton's death. More people read him now than when he was alive. The International Merton Society has chapters all around the world. Patrick Hart recently informed me that *The Intimate Merton*, which he and Jonathan Montaldo edited, is now being translated into Chinese. No doubt about it, Merton stirs people toward wonder. He did so at the very beginning of his writing career over forty years ago and does so now.

As in most things, he was ahead of his time. The poets he read and praised forty years ago are the poets that people are reading today: Lorca, Neruda, Rilke, and R. S. Thomas. He was always a good judge of writers. He corresponded with Czeslaw Milosz many years before the Polish poet won the Nobel Prize. In fact, the two men became friends. For a short time Merton actually became the poet's spiritual advisor.

Spent a beautiful summer morning reading *Striving Towards Being: The Letters of Thomas Merton and Czeslaw Milosz*. Milosz encouraged Merton to read the Carmel poet Robinson Jeffers. CM wins Merton over: "The reason I am attracted by Jeffers is probably the same I am attracted by you. Not poetry 'per se' but an effort to communicate a vision of the universe."[15]

What a compliment! And it is his very vision that brings me back to Merton again and again. I'm in good company.

Merton's vision? His gaze ventures beyond the egotistical self until it is fixed upon Christ.

Milosz confesses to Merton, "So my activity is socially determined and I cannot claim solitude. But without a certain amount of solitude and without texts of contemplatives I become very soon sterile."[16]

How true that is for many of us. A vicarious trip to Merton's abbey through his writing is better than nothing. More than that, it is a swim in a pure mountain stream. One feels refreshed and cleansed—not a bad feeling. That's the way I feel every time I read Merton!

The pope's name reminds me of Merton's brother, John Paul. Merton loved his brother but always felt guilty about his cavalier treatment of his kid sibling who trailed him constantly when they were growing up. Tom chased him away with stones. Typical brotherly behavior, but Merton suffered a nagging guilt for rejecting his brother. His beautiful poem about his brother's death, "FOR MY BROTHER: REPORTED MISSING IN ACTION, 1943," is a tribute to John Paul and radiant with fraternal love. Who could ever forget the opening verses,

> Sweet brother, if I do not sleep
> My eyes are flowers for your tomb.[17]

I'm reminded of my own brother and his death in his thirties. What is agonizing is the lost potential, for one never knows what could have been. So one learns to accept God's will. My brother Kevin, however, left a legacy in four beautiful children. That is a consolation I have but Merton didn't.

Merton did have the satisfaction of seeing his brother convert to Catholicism. That meant a lot to him.

I won't be able at the retreat to give Merton's complete biography. Just the highlights. But to choose the highlights, that's no easy matter. Certainly no more than half an hour of biography. Perhaps I should offer an intellectual biography—instead of a facts and events bio—because Merton's life centered so profoundly around the authors he was reading. For instance, he may never have converted if he hadn't read Gilson's *The Spirit of Medieval Philosophy* and Maritain's *Art and Scholasticism.*

Events or books? I also must be careful not to become bogged down by minutiae or I'll lose my audience.

To keep before me always: What does Merton say to us about the spiritual life?

Merton's litmus test of the contemplative life is love. The journey inward must pass through the center to God and then outward toward others in love.

Too many people embark on the inner journey and dead-end in narcissism. It almost happened to Merton; signs of it appear in his first *Seeds of Contemplation* with his holier-than-thou and Catholic triumphalist attitude. He recognized the all-knowing, holy monk persona and quickly discarded it. Merton became ruthless about tearing off the false masks he'd donned. He could do so because he closely examined himself every day. And he recorded it!

It requires high courage to look into the mirror of our souls, daily.

I have chosen the retreat poems. Each retreatant will receive a packet of twelve poems for reading and reflection. Each poem illuminates some aspect of Merton's life, from his early days as a monk right up to the mid-1960s; thus, I combine poetry and biography, which solves, to a degree, my biographical question.

Poems:

A Letter to My Friends on Entering the Monastery of
Our Lady, 1941
Trappists Working
The Biography

After the Night Office—Gethsemani Abbey
The Reader
Whether There Is Enjoyment in Bitterness
In Silence
Stranger
Grace's House
Night-Flowering Cactus
Love Winter When the Plant Says Nothing

Jonathan Montaldo's essay, "Loving Winter When the Plant Says Nothing: Thomas Merton's Spirituality in His Private Journals," is wise and inspiring. I tend to romanticize Merton, forever canonizing him in my own mind. Jonathan's realism about Merton brings me back to earth. He reminds all Merton readers that in many ways Merton failed. But he didn't allow his failures to defeat him; thus, he learned one of life's great lessons: humility.

T. S. Eliot also learned a similar lesson: The spiritual journey is founded in love and paved in humility. An endless, infinite humility.

Browsing through Merton's journal *A Search for Solitude* after my breakfast of coffee and toast, I came across Merton's entry for August 25, 1958: "The grip the *present* has on me. That is the one thing that has grown most noticeably in the spiritual life—nothing much else has."[18] An astonishing confession from a monk of seventeen years. Not a holier man. Not purer or sincerer or kinder or humbler. But he abides in the present.

Yet this is the very thing that all mystics and poets seek: The Holy Now moment.

Poetry is grounded in pure experience. Its perennial message is "Attention!"

Attention to the Now is at the heart of the contemplative life. For many years I've entertained a private suspicion that if I were more attentive to the Now, I'd be granted "a tremor of bliss, a wink of heaven, a whisper."[19] It's a notion I still believe in.

Attention is as arduous as weight-lifting, but the more we do it, the easier it gets. It is a matter of will and exercise.

This moment I have on my desk a copy of Brother Lawrence's *Practice of the Presence of God.* It's a small blue book about the size of my palm, a gift of a colleague. I open it and read its raised print: Bradford Smith, Shaftsbury, Vermont. Bradford Smith, grandfather of my colleague, was a Quaker scholar, and I'm not surprised Brother Lawrence spoke to him. Like Merton, Brother Lawrence lived the holiness of the Now moment in his kitchen amidst the clanging of his pots and pans.

I am more attentive to the Now, better now at fifty-three years of age than at twenty-three. But not by a whole lot!

Walking every day is good for my health, for my high blood pressure, but I find excuses for not embarking on my daily stroll. Is it laziness or just plain stubbornness?

A spiritual immaturity seems to prevent me from becoming more attuned to the present. Helplessly, I see myself caught up in diversion, digression, and, yes, say it: delusion.

I must gently become attentive to God who is present Now. I was inspired by Simone Weil when I composed this poem:

Lord,

>
> Teach me to be attentive
> To all your vestiges:
> To the first light,
> To the waking bird,
> To the leaf's rustle and the rain's drop,
> To the scent of water and the sky's hue
>> and the rise of the wind;

Lord,

> Teach me to be so attentive that
> I shall hear the first flakes of the snow's fall.

Merton describes his writing as meditating on paper. I understand, for it's what I do. The blank page helps me to focus and invites me to express my thoughts as simply as I can. Writing requires acute attention. Which entails a forgetting of the ego—for a time. Bad writing is fraught with egotism. The best writing is egoless, like that of Shakespeare and T. S. Eliot.

My friend Jack says there's just too much of Merton to read. He finds it all intimidating. Some of my retreatants will feel the same way. To counter such anxiety, I must be careful not to cover too much ground. My goodness, it's only a one-day retreat! Tunnel vision is the way to go. Of course, since it is a poetry retreat, I have already chosen a lens.

Today I reread Merton's comments about the fourteenth-century mystic Julian of Norwich. Again Merton was ahead of everyone. Julian is the most popular of today's medieval mystics, a close second is Hildegard of Bingen. Merton would have loved Hildegard, especially her joy in nature. He himself became quite a naturalist at the end of his life. Living in his hermitage, he was acutely aware of birds, snakes, deer, sunrise, clouds, rain, mist, heat, cold—much like the Chinese sages he admired.

Merton's attention to nature's beauty is surely rooted in his love of Gerard Manley Hopkins's verse that praises nature's "inscape," the essential quality of an object:

> The world is charged with the grandeur of God.
> It will flame out, like shining from shook foil.
> It gathers to a greatness, like the ooze of oil
> Crushed.[20]

Merton searched for the inscape of things. We see this particularly in his journal *A Vow of Conversation* and especially in his descriptions of deer. By long looking he hoped to penetrate through the appearance of reality to the "thisness" of what he beheld.

Rilke, a favorite poet of Merton's, says long gazing leads to "inseeing." One experiences an object from the inside looking out because subject and object become one.

Am I not seeking an "inseeing" with Merton?

> When I was young I turned to poetry not to embrace
> reality but to escape it. Now as a person over fifty...I
> turn to poetry for different reasons. Rarely do I desire to
> escape reality. On the contrary I want to enfold it, to
> become one with the immediate, to live acutely in the
> Present Moment, in the manner of the mystics and
> poets. Too often in my life I've chastised myself for not
> living intensely, for being inattentive to life's splendid
> and various details.

I wrote this paragraph over a year ago. I am now of the age
Merton was when he accidentally died of electrocution in
Bangkok in 1968. I have grown more attentive. Of that I am
certain. Most noticeably I look at beauty, the beauty of my
mother's kind face, of nature, of art, of music, of literature. As
a means for growing in attentiveness, reading is at the top of
my list. To read attentively means attention to details. Yes, I
definitely see the details of life more clearly.

Merton says of reading:

> Reading ought to be an act of homage to the God of all
> truth. We open our hearts to woods that reflect the real-
> ity He has created or the greater Reality which He is. It
> is also an act of humility and reverence towards other
> men who are the instruments by which God communi-
> cated His truth to us.[21]

What details in my reading of Merton have I skimmed over,
or perhaps ignored? What Merton poem is truly a gem, but I
haven't paid any attention to it? Something to think about...

I've not given enough attention to Merton's poem "Hagia Sophia." It is a breakthrough prose-poem because Merton faces what he called his "refusal of women." He candidly admits in his later journals that he mistreated women, some of whom he really loved. But the poem is too long and would require too much explication to include in the retreat handout.

Is it too facile to say that it is not "hatred" of women that plagued Merton, but fear that they'd reject him? Is it possible that he viewed his mother's death when he was only six as a rejection? Would Merton's life have been quite different if his mother had allowed him a last few visits to her in the hospital instead of her sending him a letter?

I am haunted by the image of the six-year-old Merton, sitting in a rain-streaked car outside the hospital where his mother is dying.

When Merton meets and falls in love with his nurse M., his "refusal of women" dissolves. John Howard Griffin sensitively addresses Merton's relationship with M. in *Follow the Ecstasy.* Yet there are so many Catholics who reject Merton for his "affair." They say he wasn't faithful to his vows (how do they know?). When people object to Merton's behavior, I simply remind them that during the 1960s and 1970s thousands of Catholics departed from convents, rectories, and seminaries. Vows or no vows, with or without dispensations.

Merton didn't depart. He remained a monk and a priest within his Cistercian order. Simple fact.

I've taken down from my shelf one of my most precious books, Thomas Merton's *Eighteen Poems*. In 1966 he had entrusted these poems to a friend with the request that they were not to be published until after his death. These are the poems Merton wrote for M.

When I purchased the book, I considered it an extravagance. I really couldn't afford it; in fact, it remains the most expensive book I've ever bought. I am glad now, however, that it rests on my shelf. Every once in a while, like today, I'll take it in my hands and enjoy its touch, and slide the book from its case and open to its rich Arches pages. Then to read the verse where I meet a Merton naked of masks: Merton, the man in love.

Perhaps I should include one of his love poems in my retreat handout. Why shouldn't I? I like "I Always Obey My Nurse."

> I always obey my nurse
> I always care
> For wound and fracture
> Because I am always broken
> I obey my nurse[22]

A poignant poem because Merton is intensely aware that he is broken in more ways than one, and he humbly shares his brokenness with the reader. M.'s love for the broken Merton will "break" him more, breakage that is paradoxically his cure, because she shatters his mask: his conviction that he is unlovable.

I am now reading the last page of *Eighteen Poems*:

> The text for this book was set by hand in Spectrum types. Two hundred fifty copies were printed by letterpress on Arches text paper at The Yolla Bolly Press during September and October of 1985, and were bound at The Schuberth Bookbindery.
>
> This is copy number 208.[23]

Sunday morning. Reread Merton's essay "Poetry and Contemplation: Reappraisal." Merton's humility is so refreshing. The first version of this essay was included at the end of his volume of verse, *Figures for an Apocalypse*. Later, he realized he'd been again a victim of dualism and admits to "my wrong-headed propositions." I know of no writer so openly willing to admit error. Compare Merton to someone like the poet Ezra Pound who chose to live his life in silence rather that admit he was egregiously wrong about so many things.

Merton learned to accept the fact that if God so wills it, anyone can indeed be a contemplative and a poet at the same time. (Merton himself was the living proof!) Merton had compartmentalized contemplation and the composition of verse, one being sacred and the other somehow profane. Several years later he was a wiser man. He writes, "Contemplation is not to be thought of as a separate department of life, cut off from all man's other interests and superseding them. It is the very fullness of a fully integrated life. It is the crown of life and of all life's activities."[24] The key word here is "integrated." Merton truly became more and more integrated the longer he remained in Gethsemani.

Later in the essay he says all poets are contemplative "in some degree." Surely he is being guarded, knowing full well the censors will read what he writes. But the fact of the matter is that all poets *must* be contemplative, otherwise verse doesn't come into being.

And I would further argue that serious readers of poetry are contemplatives. To plumb the depths of verse a person must be willing to take a journey toward meaning. This requires silence and solitude with the text. The poem in effect becomes the reader's *lectio divina*. Reader becomes monk, if only for a brief time. But it is worth it when the reader achieves insights that not only help him toward a deeper understanding of the poem, but also when he gains insights into his own life. The great value of reading verse is that it enhances our lives with beauty and knowledge, especially self-knowledge.

George Steiner says that literature possesses the power to "transmute" our lives.[25] I agree. For instance, I have no idea how the poetry retreat will affect the lives of those who attend. It is very possible that something in Merton's verse will touch a retreatant to the point that his or her life is transformed.

One verse has the power to accomplish this. Even one word.

I think of Emily Dickinson's wise little poem:

A word is dead
When it is said,
Some say.
I say it just
Begins to live
That day.[26]

Merton talks about the essential dignity of the aesthetic experience. When he was living in New York City, he often visited the Metropolitan Museum of Art. Standing before a painting by Fra Angelico, he realized that gazing upon great art, studying and appreciating its beauty, is similar to prayer. His insight occurred about the same time Simone Weil arrived at her conclusion: Attention to beauty is akin to prayer.

Another synchronicity: While reading Simone Weil, Merton was astonished to discover that his former guardian Tom Bennet served as Weil's physician. Dr. Bennet cleared up the mess of Merton's fathering a child out of wedlock. It was he who advised the young man to start over—in America.

God works in mysterious ways!

Merton's grading of his books:

Awful: *What Are These Wounds?*

Very Poor: *Exile Ends in Glory*

Poor: *Figures for an Apocalypse*

Less Good: *Man in a Divided Sea; Bread in the Wilderness; Ascent to Truth; The Last of the Fathers; Living Bread, Spiritual Direction & Meditation; Life and Holiness*

41

Good: *No Man Is an Island; The Strange Islands; Seeds of Destruction, Seasons of Celebration*

Better: *Thirty Poems; The Seven Storey Mountain; Seeds of Contemplation; Tears of the Blind Lions; Sign of Jonas; The Silent Life, Thoughts in Solitude; Wisdom of the Desert; Disputed Questions; New Seeds of Contemplation; Chuang Tzu; Emblems of a Season of Fury; Conjectures of a Guilty Bystander*

Best: None named.[27]

I'm happy that he rates his verse fairly. Three of his volumes of poetry make the Better category. I think he's a bit harsh on *Ascent to Truth*. I think it serves as a good introduction to John of the Cross's *Via Negativa*.

I'm strolling through Merton's letters. Merton's friend, correspondent, and fellow Trappist Basil Pennington once said to the Massachusetts Merton Chapter of the International Merton Society that the best way to know Merton was to read his letters. He said the letters were for the most part quickly written so that we have a spontaneous Merton before us.

I don't usually think of Merton as unspontaneous, but as Jung says, we all wear personae. Masks are necessary; they are protective covering, or else the world would make mincemeat of us. The important thing is not to become identified with the mask; the mask has nothing to do with the True Self.

After reading Merton's letters, I'm inspired to write a letter to him. I'll write it quickly and see what comes of it: Me without a mask!

Dear Thomas Merton,

I'm giving a poetry retreat centered on you. You must be aware that many people turn to you for spiritual guidance and sustenance. I've done so since I was a teenager. You've helped me become, I firmly believe, a better Christian. I can't imagine anyone receiving a greater compliment. I mean if someone, anyone for that matter, said that to me, I'd feel my life was not lived in vain.

Thank you for all the inspiration you've showered upon me through your writing. As an English teacher, I'm not as intimidated by poetry as many people are. Your poetry not only illuminates your monastic perspective, but it grapples with issues that prevent us from living intense and full lives. Some of your poems, I must admit, baffle me. Some I flat out don't understand, but I hope after spending the summer reading your collected poems, I'll penetrate the more obscure verse, especially that of *"The Geography of Lograire."*

Yes, you're my companion for the summer. You and me every day. That's how people get to know each other: hanging out and listening and watching. I'm watching you closely, not because I think you're strange or anything like that—though lots of people think monks are a bit crazy!—but because I think you've got the skinny on modern life. See, like you, I don't think we're here on earth to accumulate things or seek status or maintain fat bank accounts. I believe our purpose in life is a spiritual one: to know and to love God and to love our neighbor. It's easy to write such things, but hard to live them. You did it, and that's why so many of us admire you. You gave up everything to "disappear into God." You sacrificed what many consider the "good things" of life:

43

money, good food and drink, ambition, marriage, a family. To do so for God is heroic.

Few feel comfortable with being called a hero, but I say it from my heart: You are a model of what I'd like to become, a man committed to belief and willing to sacrifice for that belief.

I believe that poetry possesses the power to inspire people to live better lives, even amazing lives. This is because poetry often makes me want to shout with joy. It exhorts me to drink as much of life's beauty as I can. It inspires me to live beautifully in and through God.

Unfortunately, many people haven't a clue about poetry's power, even though it's all there for their taking. So as a man in his fifties, I've decided to devote my life to conducting poetry retreats. My first retreat is dedicated to you. Your verse says important things about the inner life. Although many already know you through your prose, they'll be surprised to discover Merton the poet, how you manage a marriage of contemplation and poetry, an integration achieved in beautiful, insightful, and life-enhancing verse.

Besides introducing people to your verse, I hope to help readers overcome their general fear of poetry. Some look upon verse as they do mathematics, fearing its difficulty and sometime obscurity. They're also afraid of poetry's intimacy. Let's face it: Poets stand nude before their readers. That takes courage and humility for both the poets and the readers, since more than likely they'll see themselves in poetry. Which is good, because verse leads to greater self-knowledge, a somewhat scary affair for most of us.

I'm rambling, so let me end this letter. If it's not too much to ask, will you hang around for a while this summer? After that I'll never ask for such a prolonged visitation. You see, this poetry retreat is making me nervous. I mean, who am I to give a Merton retreat! But I can do it with a little help from a friend. Thanks!

There was a good amount of Catholic triumphalism in Merton's early verse. Surely the ardor of a new convert. In his poem "A Letter to My Friends," that and his *contemptus mundi* are blatant. Like a love-struck young man, he feels no other woman can equal his two ladies: Mother Church and the Monastery of Our Lady of Gethsemani. Thus nothing in the world outside the monastic enclosure can match the beauty within it. He writes:

> These sheds and cloisters,
> The very stones and beams are all befriended
> By cleaner sun, by rarer birds, by lovelier flowers.[28]

Obviously a happy monk, Merton lets his friends know it. A little bragging, but done in the spirit of love. Yet it's a happiness founded upon rejection. The inside/outside mentality is divisive; it represents the split within Merton himself. He has not integrated the old Merton with the new; in short, he hasn't forgiven himself of his past. The giveaway is the phrase "cleaner sun." I wanted to write "clearer sun"; that makes more sense in writing about the sun that may be obscured by clouds, mist, smoke, etc. But here there is the hint of the uncleanness of sin.

He needs to "befriend" himself, not so much his friends whom he already loves and accepts. The cure for the split in himself is self-acceptance.

In "Trappists Working" Merton's world is centered on *Ora et Labora*, prayer and work. All things praise God, including the saws that "sing holy sonnets in the world of timber."[29]

Everything about the farm is holy. Well, of course. It's not just any farm, but a Trappist farm. Therefore everything contained within its sacred borders is holy, including the meanest of things, saws. Again, the ardor of a convert.

It's easy for Merton to declare Gethsemani sacred ground, but to declare the outside as sacred—that declaration is harder for Merton. It will come, but only after Merton becomes more comfortable with himself. The Louisville Vision has to be a sign of the breakthrough.

Some Merton aficionados say they're tired of hearing people quote the Louisville Vision. That it's become a cliché. Funny, I never weary of hearing about Lady Julian's hazelnut or her "All manner of things shall be well," or St. Francis kissing the leper or Simone Weil's possession by Christ when she heard Gregorian chant at Solesme. These are numinous moments in the lives of extraordinary people and hearing them over and over is like listening to Bach or Mozart. So why should I tire of hearing that Merton loves his brothers and sisters?

Received a nice plug for my books from Marci Whitney, publisher of *Christianity and the Arts*. Marci published my essay on the Catholic poet Anne Porter. Mrs. Porter is now in her late eighties and still composing verse. She is a Catholic convert and influenced her husband, the well-known painter,

Fairfield F. Porter who, when he died, was reading Lady Julian's *Revelations of Divine Love.*

Merton loved Lady Julian. He came to prefer her to St. John of the Cross. That says volumes about his "refusal of women."

Here's the gem of a poem I missed, "When in the Soul of the Serene Disciple." I'll include it in my retreat handout. In this brief poem Merton presents his ideal self, the person of utter poverty, stripped of all. A "still man" stripped even of language because "there is no longer any need of comment."[30]

So why does Merton still need to write so many books? Because being a writer is what he is. To cease writing isn't an option for him. He can't jump out of his own skin and be something else. Born writer. His abbots wisely understood his God-given gift, encouraging him to write. (It also brought in plenty of money!)

Naturally we question whether or not he'd have been a better Trappist if he'd given up writing.

I can't answer that question. It's the same question often entertained about Gerard Manley Hopkins. But I believe Merton integrated his writing with his monastic vocation because he was never embarrassed about being a writer. Hopkins, however, never escaped his feeling that writing verse was somewhat frivolous. His "terrible sonnets" reveal this agonizing conflict. If Hopkins had been proud to be a poet, he would have been a far happier man and probably a better Jesuit.

Merton was proud and glad to be a writer, and fortunate to have abbots who perceived no contradiction in doing God's will as a monk—and as a writer.

Yet in "Serene Disciple," Merton dreams of being a man without the need to comment. We always desire what we cannot have. Such is the human condition.

Two days of rain. One day a drenching rain, the other an off-and-on drizzle. People usually dismiss these as dreary summer days, preferring the sun over rain anytime. But I like such days—good for reading and thinking.

I take down my copy of *Raids on the Unspeakable* to reread Merton's "Rain and the Rhinoceros." This is a prose poem about what the poet Samuel Hazo calls "The Holy Surprise of the Right Now."[31] Merton is "onto" the joy of the present moment. He accepts and luxuriates in the rain. He sees its beauty, he hears its joy, he feels its freshness, he tastes its Now-ness.

He delights in the smell of drenched pine needles and in the appearance of the dandelion that has "pushed itself into bloom between the smashed leaves of last summer's day lilies."[32] Pine needles and the dandelion weed: finding joy even in what is often perceived as useless.

Received an unexpected phone call from Brother Patrick Hart. He is delighted with the success of *The Intimate Merton* that he and Jonathan Montaldo edited. Translated into several languages, including Chinese, it will make Merton available to many more people. He now considers this volume a companion piece to Merton's autobiography. Kenneth Woodward of

Newsweek supports this view: "Merton's real autobiography is in his personal journals."[33]

Last summer when I visited Gethsemani, I had the opportunity to look over the manuscript. I was delighted that Merton's dreams had been indexed. Here is an area for exploration, where new insights about Merton, both the monk and the man, can be excavated.

Browsing through *The Intimate Merton*, I came across this dream, recorded Wednesday, June 22, 1966:

> I dreamt in several different ways of trying to contact M. I cannot remember what the dreams were, only that the last one, before I woke up, was that I was sending a child to the hospital to tell her that I loved her. I realized this was most unsatisfactory but there was nothing else I could do. (I was aware that the child would just go in and say "He told me today he loves you" in an embarrassed sort of way and walk out again.)[34]

A revelatory dream. I see it as tinged with a childhood memory: Merton outside the hospital where his mother was dying and his not being able to say his goodbye and his final "I love you." If Merton's mother handled her death differently, Merton may have traveled down a different road.

A simple thing to say "I love you." Or is it?

On September 2, 1966, Merton records another dream:

> I know that M. is swimming alone in one of our lakes. I am near there but I have refrained from joining her for fear of the consequences. But now I approach the lake

and see her wading in the water over there by the shore. She looks so disconsolate and alone, as if she had wasted the afternoon...I go down toward the lake dressed in my habit and wave to her that I am coming. She still looks disconsolate, unbelieving. I wish to join her, I think, even if I have to swim naked. There appears to be no one around. But as I go to her along the bank I find one of the monks sitting there in my way. I cannot get to her. At this I wake up in great distress.[35]

The dream reveals Merton's ambivalence about M. No doubt he loves her very much. But he knows in his heart that the obstacle between them is the monk sitting along the bank. That monk is Merton himself. The distress he feels on awaking is both for M. and himself. He's wasting M.'s time, for he knows in his very being that he'll never depart from his chosen vocation.

When I read about Merton and M., I am filled with compassion. Why is it that so many others are either distressed or angered? Merton is a man, and love, like death, will come when it will come. And he handled it wisely—in the end. Give the man credit!

Who said we all live in glass houses and shouldn't throw stones? An interesting play on Christ's admonition.

When *A Vow of Conversation* was published in 1988, it quickly superseded *Sign of Jonas* as my favorite journal. (*A Vow* is now included in *Learning to Love.*)

50

Today I returned to *A Vow*. It is, to borrow Sister Therese Lentfoehr's phrase, a "Zen transparent" journal. Just strolling through it, I came across beautiful haiku-like entries:

1964:

January 3: Warm wind. Bright sun. Melting snow. Water off the roof splashing in all the buckets around the hermitage.

February 7: Cold wind, dark sky, and sleet.

April 28: A bright delightful day washed clean of smoke and dust by two days' rain. Brilliant sky, bird song, hills clothed in their green sweaters.

August 24: A wonderful sky all day, beginning with the abstract expressionist Jackson Pollock dawn. Scores of streaks and tiny blue-gray clouds flung like blotches all over it.

September 12: Tiny delicate fishbones of clouds in the sky.

November 2: Birds. A titmouse was swinging and playing in the dry weeds by the monastery woodshed. A beautiful, small, trim being.

November 24: In the night, a rumpled thin skin of cloud covered the skies, not totally darkening the moon.

November 30: Night. Zero cold. Frozen leaves crackling like glass under my feet on the path through the woods.

1965:

January 17: Brilliant night, deep snow, sparkling in the moon.

January 31: The beautiful jeweled shining of honey in the lamplight. Festival!

February 11: Nightfall. Wind from the west. The porch shines with rain and low dark rags of clouds blow over the valley.

March 19: Bright, full moon. Absolute silence of the moon-lit valley.

April 18, Easter Sunday: The peace and beauty of Easter morning! Sunrise, deep green grass, soft winds, the woods turning green on the hills across the valley and here too.

May 20: Gray dawn, and a blood-red sun furious among the pines.

September 6: Magenta mist outside the windows. A cock crows over at Boone's farm.[36]

Poetry-like entries are scattered throughout the diary. His last entry in *A Vow*, describing his sighting of a deer, to be read completely to be appreciated. Merton at his most Rilkean.

I was never threatened by Merton's delving into Zen. Many of my Catholic friends remain uncomfortable with it. And then the crazy rumors that Merton was leaving the church to become a Zen Buddhist. Nonsense!

He reached out to the East in an attempt to discover common contemplative ground. Then his journey to the East. Barefoot in the wet grass and sand of Colombo, he reverently stood before the Polonnaruwa Buddhas and was "jerked clean" out of himself.

It was an "aesthetic illumination," he writes, that paradoxically says everything and says nothing. His life had come full circle. Within his own being he had experienced a marriage of opposites.

Six days later, stepping wet from a shower, he contacted a faulty fan and was electrocuted.

For a time I was suspicious about the manner of Merton's death. But by all accounts it was a terrible accident; nothing of a dubious nature occurred. His body was returned to America for burial at Gethsemani, on an aircraft carrying dead GIs from Vietnam.

It was a trip down memory lane to dust off and open Merton's *Mystics and Zen Masters*. In the 1970s my two mentors were Merton and Alan Watts. Zen was important to me in my search for a direct grasp of reality. I meditated, as did millions of others, and I hoped for what the Buddhists call *satori*, or illumination. And I searched, as did Merton, for the common ground between East and West.

Alan Watts came to reject his Christian background, perhaps a fatal error for him. Fatal because his early death might have been the result of his failure to individuate within Zen Buddhism. That and his adoption of an "anything goes" morality.

Merton's goal, however, was to integrate what Buddhism offered concerning the search for the True Self. I believe he was indeed on the right path. Both Christianity and Buddhism address suffering; both point toward a compassionate and loving relationship with the world, a world that must be grasped purely in the Now moment.

Perhaps the word *grasp* is too aggressive a metaphor. Reality is not so much grasped as it is realized; we become aware of it, attentive to its presence *now.* The older I become, as I've said before, the more I'm convinced that the secret of the spiritual life lies in the act of attention. I say "act" because choice is definitely involved. We choose to be attentive or inattentive.

Obeying an early morning whim after my coffee, I opened Alan Watts's autobiography to reread his assessment of Merton: "Thomas Merton, for example, really understood what Zen is all about, and wrote most admirably of Chuang-tzu's Taoism."[37]

Of his own books, Merton's favorite was *The Way of Chuang Tzu*.

As an autobiography Watts's *In My Own Way* isn't as great as Merton's *The Seven Storey Mountain*. But it's an important and riveting account of another modern man in search of his soul. Watts would have been wise, however, to have considered Carl Jung's admonition that to achieve psychological and spiritual wholeness one must individuate within one's own culture. In the end Watts rejected his cultural roots, a rejection that sadly ended in his alcoholism. How sad for a former Anglican priest. Yet I still think his *Behold the Spirit* is an inspiring Christian book. And within its covers I first came across the name of Carl Jung who served an important role in my young adulthood.

Both Watts and Merton sat at the feet of D. T. Suzuki. They considered him a profoundly enlightened man. And in their own ways both men achieved rare insights about the spiritual life. Did they achieve enlightenment? According to the Japanese philosopher Kitaro Nishida's definition of enlightenment, they indeed were enlightened men by the mere fact that they sought it.

Zen = egolessness.

Christ said, "In losing yourself you will find yourself." Merton writes that *kenosis*, self-emptying, is the purpose of contemplation. To empty ourselves for Christ's indwelling.

Merton and Watts were attracted to Chuang Tzu's Taoism. They pursued "pure experience." Both men were happy when they wrote their books on Chuang Tzu. During the composition of his book, Merton established a deep friendship with John Wu, a Chinese scholar. While writing his last book, *Tao: The Watercourse Way*, Watts established a life-enhancing friendship with Al Chung-liang Huang, who edited *Watercourse Way* at Watts's death.

Although Merton was a gregarious explorer of the human condition, he never presented himself as a man with all the answers. His humble bow to the East is proof of this. I well understand his reverence for the East, for Buddhism taught me about the vital role of attention in the spiritual life. That is what both the East and Simone Weil have taught me.

Merton's humility in regard to his verse is touching. When he was told that T. S. Eliot considered his poetry "too hit or miss," Merton was crushed and almost renounced verse for good. He came into his own, however, when he wrote "Elias: Variations on a Theme." He stripped his poetic line to the bare essential, mirroring his monastic asceticism.

I had to learn the same lesson in regard to writing: Less is more. My early writing was a purple prose that now makes me cringe. My ego was there for all to view.

Merton's prose is lucid and spare. If I had to compare him to anyone, it would be Hemingway whose prose style is also simple and spare. As a young man, Merton had desperately wanted to be a novelist and ended up being famous as a spiritual writer. Hemingway was a novelist who possessed a spiritual nature, yet he ignored that aspect of himself. However, Santiago's spirituality in *The Old Man and the Sea* is radiant; the old man's narrative is a watery way of the cross. If Hemingway had searched within himself more deeply, he may have found the wholeness that escaped him.

In his poem "An Elegy for Ernest Hemingway," Merton summarizes Hemingway's life as a search of "that brave illusion: the adventurous self."[38]

Two opposite ways of life: Merton chose sacrifice of the self. Hemingway chose aggrandizement of the self. But in the end Hemingway hated the self he created. He lost sight of the fact that it was just a mask. One doesn't have to kill oneself to strip away a mask; one divests oneself of it, by taking an honest look in the mirror.

Why is something as simple as introspection so difficult? Stripping ourselves of illusions is like death: The known is sacrificed in order to enter the unknown. And *terra incognita* is always a bit terrifying.

Merton learned to love the world compassionately. Hemingway needed to conquer the world; thus the persona of the macho hunter. Both men turned to John Donne for book titles: Merton's *No Man Is an Island* and Hemingway's *For Whom the Bell Tolls.* Life and death. A monk killed by electrocution and a novelist killed by his own hand.

Sunday morning. I just listened to Merton's taped lecture on William Faulkner's short story "The Bear." It is an eloquent commentary on the spiritual life. Hearing his voice is a joy, a lively, elegant voice fraught with his enthusiasm for fine writing and for a "sapiential" reading of literature. By this he meant a reading that searches for the wisdom implanted throughout the classics.

The story of bear-hunting parallels our search for God. The young boy Ike must successfully pass through various rites of passage before he's permitted a sighting of the bear. Merton, aware of his monastic audience, correlates the hunt with the monastic passages of postulancy and novitiate: simple to solemn vows.

In the beginning, the boy hears only the various sounds of the forest; later he will see the bear's footprint. Further on when a woodpecker becomes silent, he knows the bear is looking at him, but he himself has yet to see the bear.

The spiritual life is similar. We hear God's still, small voice, and we continue to listen more intently and hope for a divine glimpse later. We pray for it, but knowing that God sees us and hears us is often sufficient.

Then one day, after Ike has learned all the hunting skills, he enters the woods without his gun. No sight of the bear. So he "relinquishes" himself further to the wilderness by divesting himself of watch, compass, and a stick, brought along for snakes. He enters more deeply into the unknown. Now lost, he sits on a log and looks down to find Old Ben's footprint, so freshly made, it fills with water. Then Ike sees the bear. He couldn't have predicted or planned it, or mapped it. His seeing just happens—and yet his whole life was a preparation for such an event.

Merton is obviously overwhelmed by the story's power and says it's as valuable to monks as all the monastery's shelves of ascetical and mystical theology.

In his lecture on Faulkner, Merton emphasizes the utter importance of "intense awareness." Attention, he says, is the sine qua non of the spiritual journey. Except for that, all methods and all paths in the end become "useless."

Ike strips himself of objects employed to measure time, give direction, and offer protection; he is left only with his power of attention. And because he is intensely attentive and followed the footprints, he is gifted with seeing the bear.

If I am attentive to Merton, follow all the footprints—and he left plenty—perhaps I'll be granted a glimpse of the real Merton.

Then what?

Later when Ike has an opportunity to kill Old Ben, he can't do it. To help Ike understand why, his father reaches for Keats's poetry and reads "Ode on a Grecian Urn" to his son—twice. Ike gradually understands why his father read the poem to him. He departs knowing something about life and the pursuit of truth and beauty. He has won a portion of life's wisdom.

Poetry is the language of the numinous. That's why Merton never gave it up, even though he knew he wasn't in the same league as Eliot or Rilke.

Ike entered the forest alone since the inner journey is a solitary one. Merton understood the profound existential dread of such aloneness because it entails facing our own nothingness.

We are all hunters of the Divine.

I returned to Merton's *Zen and the Birds of Appetite*, which has a remarkable essay on the Japanese philosopher Kitaro Neshida. It has taken me a while to grasp how Merton differentiates between Zen and Christian nothingness. Older, and I hope wiser, I now see that the difference is not so much in the void but in how the void is filled—by Christ. Christ therefore is the Difference that makes a difference.

Each individual's nothingness becomes unique because of Christ. My Christ-indwelling is unlike any other, and yet very much the same! Unlike Merton's, since Merton's is unlike all others. What is similar is the fruits of Christ's dwelling within us: love and compassion. Merton says all this on the tape on Faulkner.

Visited my book dealer; he had on his shelves several of Merton's books in mint condition. And there before my eyes gleamed a fine first edition of *New Seeds of Contemplation*. Opening it, I thought it was a new book, one that had never before been handled. Seems my dealer had the good fortune to purchase a portion of James Laughlin's library. Laughlin was the founder of New Directions Press, the publisher of Merton's poetry. He had a private stash of Merton books.

Laughlin was a good friend to Merton. And Merton brought in the money! William Carlos Williams once complained to Laughlin about his disappointment in New Directions book marketing and considered leaving them. Laughlin reminded Williams that it was because of writers like Merton, who sold extremely well, that Laughlin could take chances on other poets—like Williams.

I departed from the bookshop with *New Seeds* in my hands.

"Elias: Variations on a Theme" is my favorite Merton poem, especially the fourth variation. For a long time, I was puzzled by the opening lines:

> Under the blunt pine
> I who am not sent
> Remain. The pathway dies,
> The journey has begun.[39]

But last summer I saw the light. Merton wrote the poem in a red trailer beneath a pine tree. And nearby are paths that go nowhere. That's the setting, but the symbolic significance is one I grappled with further. Why does the pathway die? That intrigued me. Then the dawn: It dies because each pilgrim paves his own path; he cannot walk another's path. If he does, he can only go so far.

We can go so far with Merton, and then arrives the time when we must proceed on our own unique journey, like Ike in "The Bear." That's not to say that Merton can't help us by offering encouragement, wisdom, and even directions. But in the end we all make our own path. Or we stop dead in our tracks and sit on the ground and wait. Yes, waiting is an important part of the journey.

That old run-down red trailer is now derelict, overgrown with vines and hidden by trees. One would think the Trappists would have preserved it in memory of Merton. Even Merton's first hermitage, St. Anne's shed, has fallen into ruin.

On the other hand, Merton's legacy is safely preserved in his books. Plaques are unnecessary.

I will recommend to my retreatants five of Merton's spiritual classics: *Seeds* and *New Seeds* as well as *No Man Is an Island, Bread in the Wilderness, and Thoughts in Solitude.* But if I had to narrow it down to one, it would be *New Seeds.* I could spend the rest of my life meditating on this one book alone. It contains the essence of Merton's thought. From the chapter in *New Seeds,* "Everything That Is, Is Holy": "There is no evil in anything created by God, nor can anything of His become an obstacle to our union with Him."[40]

From Blake and Hopkins, Merton learned that holiness surrounds us, within and without. He understood this intellectually, but for some years he lived as if he didn't believe it.

The hermitage years best illustrate his belief in the Holy Now moment. He renders the ordinary holy: chopping wood, making a fire, cooking a meal, listening to rain, saying his breviary, writing, going out to watch the deer from his porch, and so on. Because he is so exquisitely attentive to the movements of his exterior and interior life, he sees the holy in the ordinary and the ordinary in the holy.

When I was young, I wanted to be holy. Ever since I made my First Communion, the saints were held up as models. How could I forget those holy card pictures: saints with hands folded and eyes raised to heaven, which the nuns passed out when we were "good." They meant well.

The wish for holiness, if made in the right spirit, renders us holy in the instant. Furthermore, it isn't rare to meet holy people. I meet them often. I'm sure that the retreatants by the mere fact of their presence will have attained a level of holiness.

Holiness is not a Mount Everest climb because "it's there." Such ascents are ego trips. Holiness's direction is downward: down with the false self, down with egotism, down with aspirations to be "holy." Then there is the ascent: upward without effort on the wings of the Holy Spirit.

Merton says that when God touches us in the Holy Now moment,

> A door opens in the center of our being and we seem to fall through it into immense depths which, although they are infinite, are all accessible to us; all eternity seems to have become ours in this one placid and breathless contact.[41]

There are moments in our reading life that we never forget. Usually they are moments of epiphany when we see something about life that we've never comprehended before or perhaps saw but didn't understand at the time. For me one such moment occurred in college. I had read the following:

Your idea of me is fabricated with materials you have borrowed from other people and from yourself. What you think of me depends on what you think of yourself. Perhaps you create your idea of me out of material that you would like to eliminate from your own idea of yourself. Perhaps your idea of me is a reflection of what other people think of you. Or perhaps what you think of me is simply what you think I think of you.[42]

I remember being bowled over by this passage of Merton's. Who was I then? And how could I know others? Is it even possible? At the time I knew nothing of Carl Jung's theory of psychological projection. As a result I analyzed very carefully my relationships with friends and colleagues.

I did achieve insight into myself. For instance, when I once dismissed someone as arrogant, I checked myself: "How did I recognize arrogance so quickly? Perhaps I'm seeing myself in this person." At the time it was exactly the case.

To prevent the world from becoming a projection of yourself, Merton teaches, you must devote your life to stripping away false selves. That process calls for a lifetime of attentiveness.

Received in the mail today *The Merton Seasonal.* On the front cover is a photograph of the Baptistry of Corpus Christi Church in New York City where Merton was baptized into the Catholic Church in 1938. The same baptistry font served for the baptism of Terence Cooke in 1921; the font was preserved from the old Corpus Christi church demolished to build the present one. At Corpus Christi, Cardinal Cooke celebrated the funeral Mass of Father George Ford who had received Merton into the church.

The Seasonal has an insightful essay by Abbot John Eudes Bamberger, Merton's student and colleague. Bamberger also knew Father Henri Nouwen. Volumes by both men crowd my bookshelves. Merton, however, is the one I read more often because he's the deeper philosopher and theologian. Nouwen is charismatic. I once heard him preach and he was riveting, but not the intellectual Merton was.

Merton and Nouwen were both complicated in regard to their need for human contact. Merton's need for solitude, however, was greater than his need for people. On the other hand, Nouwen craved people's affirmation. He suffered from depression when he didn't receive it. In the end, Nouwen followed Bamberger's advice not to become a Trappist but to pursue a ministry of teaching, preaching, and spiritual direction.

Merton and Nouwen are both fine writers on the spiritual life. They remind me, however, of Faulkner and Hemingway. Even though both novelists received Nobel Prizes, Faulkner plunged far more deeply into the human soul than Hemingway.

The important thing is that Merton and Nouwen meet the needs of their readers, and judging by their book sales, both priests are reaching many people.

From Merton's preface to the Japanese edition of *The Seven Storey Mountain*:

Therefore, most honorable reader, it is not as an author that I would speak to you, not as a story-teller, not as a philosopher, not as a friend only; I seek to speak to you, in some way, as your own self.[43]

Perhaps the reason for my preference of Merton over Nouwen is that I see myself more often in Merton, whereas with Nouwen I can't get beyond his personality.

Nouwen was greatly impressed by Merton's Louisville Vision. He experienced a similar epiphany visiting Rochester, not far from the Abbey of Genesee in upstate New York where Nouwen temporarily adopted the Trappist life "to face my restless self."

He had entered a florist's shop:

> When I walked into a flower shop to buy some white and yellow chrysanthemums for friends in town I felt a deep love for the florist who, with a twinkle in his eye, told me that chrysanthemums were "year-round flowers," not bound to the seasons. I felt open, free, and relaxed and really enjoyed the little conversation we had on flowers, presidents, and honesty in politics.[44]

In 1976, when I first read Nouwen's *Genesee Diary*, I remember thinking how fragile Nouwen's ego was. He was easily hurt, nursing slights that were never intended. Of course, after a while he realized that the monks indeed liked him, but they weren't about to treat him any differently because he was a writer.

The opposite was true for Merton. At Gethsemani he was treated differently—because he was a best-selling writer. I wonder how much resentment that caused within the community?

My best writing ideas come to me as I walk around a nearby pond; the walk is a little over a mile and it usually takes me about twenty-five minutes. Today it occurred to me that an interesting way to offer a Merton biography is to discuss the epiphanies he experienced. There are many, but the most important are

> The trip to Rome where he first experienced Christ
> Conversion in New York
> The trip to Havana and mystical experience at Mass
> The Louisville Vision
> Polannaruwa

These are radiant, life-transforming moments. What they share in common is beauty. The beauty of Rome's Byzantine mosaics enthralled the young Merton to the point of becoming lost in their beauty. The beauty of the Mass in Havana and the singing of the young people. The beauty of Louisville's people on the city's street. The monumental Polannaruwa Buddhas, so impressive and beautiful that he was "jerked clean" out of himself.

At random I opened Henri Nouwen's last diary, *Sabbatical Journey*, and read something I'd underlined on my first reading, "The truth is that I do not feel much, if anything, when I pray."[45] He was in a spiritually arid time and suffered from physical exhaustion. He should have had a complete physical, especially a stress test for his heart. He too quickly assumed his tiredness was psychological and spiritual; he was only partially right.

Then I opened Merton's *New Seeds of Contemplation* at random and the following leapt up at me: "Prayer and love are really learned in the hour when prayer becomes impossible and your heart turns to stone."[46]

Is not my keeping this diary a kind of prayer? There are moments when I wonder why I write. But I persevere because I have found the saving word in both Merton's and Nouwen's diaries.

Both men had strong libidos. Merton was a lusty heterosexual in his youth. He fathered a child out of wedlock. He had several girlfriends. But he sacrificed marriage for God. His energy, though, was still there with him in the monastery. He fortunately had his writing as an outlet. His opus is astounding. He corresponded with more than 1800 people!

Nouwen also channeled his libido into writing. There is discussion now of his homosexuality. If he was homosexual, it makes no difference. Like Merton, he sacrificed that side of himself for God. Of course, it was no easier for him than it was for Merton to remain faithful to chastity. But the fact of the matter is that both men were men of love. And in the end what else matters?

I'm getting a little worried about who will attend my retreat. Although I've advertised on the internet and in the local newspaper and at the Dominican Priory, I haven't received any definite booking, that is, a check in the mail. The retreat house needs $35 per person (includes lunch). I need to ask for $45 just to meet expenses. Thus far, no takers (paid!), though I've had a number of people say they will attend. I just sent the down payment to hold the date. It's nonrefundable.

My nightmare is to arrive at the priory and find it empty!

Of course, it's summertime and many people are on vacation. There'll likely be a rush of registrations in early September. I'm almost sure there will be enough friends attending for me to go ahead with the retreat. "Almost sure."

In his autobiography Merton talks a lot about mortal sin. One committed mortal sin, he says, is far more horrific than any bomb. He refers to himself as a great sinner, so the reader assumes he's referring to mortal sins. Yet I remember as a high school student wondering what his great sins were. He didn't appear to be terribly Augustinian.

Of course, fearful that the complete truth might jar the sensibilities of "innocent" Catholics everywhere, the censors "cleaned up" his story. How the world has changed! Today publishers would demand all the lurid details of his life in London and Cambridge and his New York pub crawling. They'd demand to know the identity of the woman who bore his child; they'd likely launch a search for her whereabouts. All we know is that both mother and child likely died in the bombing of World War II.

How God works in mysterious ways! The Franciscans refused to admit Merton because of his "sinful" past. But, with the same knowledge of said past, the Trappists accepted him.

But, again, the world has changed. Merton might have a hard time today being accepted into the Cistercian order. Would he be able to pass their battery of tests? Or the screening board interview?

There have been a few harsh comments on Merton's entry into the Abbey of Gethsemani. One critic said he committed a "bloodless suicide." William Carlos Williams referred to it as an escapist disappearance. Both remarks are foolish. Merton tingled with life to his fingertips, and in no way was he an escapist. If there was flight in his life, it was of a different kind. He writes:

> There is only one true flight from the world; it is not an escape from conflict, anguish and suffering, but the flight from disunity and separation, to unity and peace in the love of other men.[47]

We should all be such "escapists."

Some of Merton's finest poetry is found in *The Way of Chuang Tzu*, a book he was proud of: "I have enjoyed writing this book more than any other I can remember."[48]

What is appealing about Merton's interpretations (they are not translations from the Chinese but "readings" composed from his study of two English, one French, and one German translation) is their utter simplicity and childlikeness. Here we have Chuang Tzu reduced to his essence in verse that is spare and austere but also full of life and humor. However, in the process of his "renderings" Merton reveals his own love of silence, solitude, humility, and his hope for a direct grasp of reality.

Merton is drawn to the Chinese concept of *wu-wei*—of doing nothing. More than in any other of his books, we perceive his growing distrust of spiritual methodology. His direction seems to be toward abandonment of all "ways." Epiphanies, peak experiences, moments of being will come when they will come. He notes, "When the right moment arrives, even one who seems incapable of any instruction whatever will become mysteriously aware of Tao."[49]

That's what must have happened to the young Merton when he went to Rome. Christ appeared in his life at the right time and there really was no "conscious" preparation on his part. That's what happened in Havana, in New York, and in Louisville. And finally before the Polonnaruwa Buddhas.

One's life is the way.

I am reading Merton's literary essays. Merton greatly admires Albert Camus's work. He wrote seven important essays on the Algerian-born writer. Stylistically both men employ lucidity of prose and clarity of vision. Camus sees the world as absurd. But that doesn't prevent him from loving the world and empathizing with its sufferers. Camus also advocates right action in the face of human tragedy, most evident in the character of Dr. Reiux in his novel *The Plague*.

Merton's attraction to Camus is likely the result of his feeling that he himself could only be described as a "guilty bystander." How does a monk justify his life when he has safely sequestered himself in a monastery where all his physical needs are met? How does a monk justify a life of silence and solitude when so many suffer? Is his life one of isolated indifference?

Merton's outreach to the world after the Louisville Vision is proof that he understood in a profound way that he was a member of the human family. He prayed for that family and also wrote for that family. He began to address social issues such as the Viet Nam War, the bomb, civil rights, hunger, political tyranny, and a host of other social matters. And the basis of his concern for his fellow humans was love.

Both Merton and Camus use language as a means of communication. They both understand, however, that language can be true or false. Thus, the utter importance of lucidity. Camus observes, "The human task was a humble and limited one: to find those few words by which to appease the infinite anguish of free souls."[50]

Merton offers a "few words" in *Conjectures of a Guilty Bystander*:

> In a word, if we really understood the meaning of Christianity in social life we would see it as part of the redemptive work of Christ, liberating man from misery, squalor, subhuman living conditions, economic or political slavery, ignorance, alienation.[51]

Ever humble, Merton says he has no answers, but he will still ask the questions and offer his own "conjectures."

Merton wanted to be a novelist, the kind that Camus represents, one with something important to say about the human condition. What a trilogy of novels he could have written about his life at Cambridge, at Columbia, and finally at Gethsemani.

But that was not to be his genre.

Has there ever been a good "inside" novel about monastic life? The nearest thing I can think of is John Howard Griffin's *The Devil Rides Outside*. I first came across selections of this novel in the *John Howard Griffin Reader*. Later I searched for the book but to no avail. Finally I ordered it through the internet's Alibris Web site. This novel should be better known. Griffin's young adult life—I'm assuming it's an autobiographical novel—parallels Merton's. The scenes in the French monastery are haunting. Griffin loves all things monastic, especially Gregorian chant, of which he was a well-known scholar.

No wonder Griffin and Merton became close friends.

So with all this study and reading of Merton, have I penetrated to the core of Merton's life? Do I know him better? Do I appreciate things I had before missed?

One thing I can say, Merton was haunted by "man's inhumanity to man."

I've argued that Merton steered clear of methodology in regard to spirituality. He doesn't offer us a paradigm, as Thomas Keating and Basil Pennington do with centering prayer. But Merton's "way" is always before us. His spiritual "discipline" is writing and reading. In short, Merton's prayer life is one of reading, reflection on his reading, and then the altruistic sharing of the book's radiant gist with his readers.

Writing and reading books become vocational habits in which Merton loses himself. Words and reader/writer become one in an act of attention. This is prayer.

The person on retreat holding in her hand the one book she brought with her to read: and how often I've noticed that the book is one by Merton!

What a great service Brother Patrick Hart and Jonathan Montaldo have performed for Mertonites all over the world with their flawless editing of Merton's journals in *The Intimate Merton*. I could spend the rest of my summer on this book alone and still not exhaust it.

They too see Merton's journal writing as a spiritual discipline. They write,

> Writing a journal was Merton's way of doing a poet's "heart work," a scholar's "inner work," a monk's "work of the cell." Writing a journal was the birth canal through which the myriad inner responses of his spirit to the world became enfleshed and took on a life of their own. Once born to the page, his words formed sentences with their own truth in them.
>
> He wrote journals as a spiritual discipline: he kept "vigil" through making a journal until a pattern of experience would unfold into momentary epiphanies....[52]

Further along in their introductory comment, they compare Merton's journals to an icon: "His journals reveal to him and to his reader that his life was no metaphor for mastery but rather an icon for spiritual mastery's salvific opposite: poverty of spirit."[53]

I have lived with Merton's iconic journals now for five weeks. Merton doesn't say he has the answers. But he knows the questions by heart and has his own vital "hints and guesses" as to answers. And that for me is sufficient.

Opened Michael Mott's biography of Merton, out of which fell a letter from Denise Levertov. I thought I'd lost this letter forever. She answered my query about how much Merton influenced her verse. She denied any influence, but Merton's prose work, she admitted, meant much to her.

Merton admired her verse. It's likely she may have influenced him. Her poetic line is stark, the way Merton's became.

Of the several biographies of Merton I will recommend to the retreatants Mott's and Shannon's. The others are a bit superficial, but they too have their value. For instance Monica Furlong's biography was the first to report Merton's fathering a child when he was at Cambridge. That opened the door for a complete revaluation of Merton the monk and Merton the man.

But really, what did it reveal except that Merton was so very human like all of us?

Reading *The New Man*. I have underestimated this book. It deserves to be rated with Merton's best spiritual writing. It is the most overtly Christ-centered of his books. Merton writes, "But if my true spiritual identity is found in my identification with Christ, then to know myself fully, I must know Christ."[54]

When I analyze my own reasons for turning to Merton I have to admit to myself that it was usually a dissatisfaction with the person I was or had become. I indeed wanted to be a "new man": more integrated, more peaceful, a more sensitive person in my relationships with my family, friends, and colleagues.

In short, I wanted to be more Christ-like.

The spiritual life is often rooted in our lack of peace; thus, we seek the peace that surpasses understanding: Christ's peace.

Merton's *The Road to Joy: Letters to New and Old Friends* is a joy to read. His letters to John Howard Griffin are particularly touching in their tender solicitude concerning Griffin's precarious health. He reminds Griffin not to forget to take his insulin. Griffin encouraged Merton's interest in photography. Merton's joy over his own photos is like that of a kid with a new toy. And when Griffin sends him a new camera, Merton is ecstatic. "It is fabulous. What a joy of a thing to work with."[55]

Just read Merton's letters to Lax. Merton is totally himself with Lax. He shares with his buddy his astonishing epiphany at St. Francis church in Havana, which he includes in his autobiography, though in a more developed passage. He says in a letter,

> Also it come to me in St. Francis church in Havana with a great shock that nearly stopped my breath that right in front of me was the whole entirety of heaven with the big stadium full of saints Dante describes in the last cantos of Paradise beholding in their midst the immense light of God. It wasn't anything like seeing anything with your eyes, but it was a sudden apprehension of a

75

clear and absolute truth so completely certain that I
went right up clean through the roof of the church like a
rocket.[56]

In his autobiography, Merton writes, "It was as if I had been
suddenly illuminated by being blinded by the manifestation
of God's presence."[57]

The letters between Merton and his poetry publisher,
James Laughlin, are a testament to friendship. Both were tal-
ented and decent men, both devoted to poetry. It was Laughlin who put together Merton's final work, *The Asian Journal.* For
Laughlin, it was a labor of love.

Laughlin believed Merton was finally graced with a mystical experience while standing before the Buddhas of Polonnaruwa. He writes: "If you read the end of Merton's Asian
Journal—when he got to Polonnaruwa in Ceylon—I think
you will be convinced, as I was, that he finally had his great
mystical experience there."[58] He later says how appropriate it
was for Merton that his vision came through his ecumenism
and not in the isolation of a Catholic monastery.

Although I agree completely with JL, I believe that Merton
did indeed have a mystical experience in Havana while at
Mass in the church of St. Francis. Odd that more people
aren't aware of it.

In his "Portrait of Merton" placed at the end of the letters,
Laughlin offers a charming remembrance of his friend. On his
visits to Gethsemani, he'd pick Merton up at the monastery
gate; Merton would be dressed in an old bishop's suit, looking
very ecclesiastical. Five minutes outside the abbey enclosure,

Merton would jump out of the car to change into jeans, old sweater, and beret. For the rest of the day, discussion of books and ideas was nonstop.

James Laughlin was delighted to have Merton in his stable of authors. *Seeds of Contemplation* was a huge money-maker for his small publishing house New Directions Press, founded with his family's money. After Ezra Pound dismissed his poetry, Laughlin decided that if he couldn't be a poet, he'd still hang around them, help them have their work published.

Laughlin thought Merton's early verse too pious, too facile. The change for the better occurred with *The Strange Islands*, the volume with "Elias: Variations on a Theme." He also holds in high esteem Merton's last verse, *The Geography of Lograire.* That is one Merton book I cannot take to. Perhaps I'm just not ready for it. I tried it again last night, and I was thoroughly baffled. And there was nothing in the verse to make me want to crack it. Funny, I can read anything else by Merton and enjoy it, but not this. Yet I love his other late poetry, *Eighteen Poems*.

Another cloudy day with the prospect of rain. The weatherman calls this the "summer that wasn't." I feel bad for all those vacationers who paid the big bucks for the cottage on the Cape or the house on Nantucket. My neighbor is back early from Martha's Vineyard. The island, she says, is "enshrouded in mist." Good title for a romantic novel.

In "A Letter on the Contemplative Life" Merton states succinctly and briefly why he entered the monastery:

It is true that when I came to this monastery where I am, I came in revolt against the meaningless confusion of a life in which there was so much activity, so much movement, so much useless talk, so much superficial and needless stimulation, that I could not remember who I was.[59]

He was referring to the early 1940s. How would Merton react to our world today with its ubiquitous talking heads, cable television, MTV, and cell phones?

Merton says that the only real message the contemplative has for the world is that "God loves you." We need contemplatives to remind us that God indeed loves us, is present, and dwells within us.

Just finished Frank Lentricchia's *The Edge of Night: A Confession*. The most intriguing portion of his "confession" is his visit to Mepkin Abbey, a Trappist monastery in South Carolina. He falls in love with the place. Passing through the gates, he says, is like entering "another intensity" where he meets a "thingish presence."[60] Lentricchia doesn't like to use the word *God*. Actually says he doesn't believe in God. So why is he at a monastery?

He also resists Thomas Merton's books, although he did purchase a number of them. He gives up on Merton's autobiography after merely twenty pages, but eats up Merton's contemplative books, "these books were short and lyrically knotty and uncluttered by mundane autobiography. I ate them up. Books about becoming empty; books about the struggle to defeat distraction."[61]

He doesn't know it yet (finally admits it toward the end), but he's hooked on Merton.

This is important for me, although it really shouldn't matter, that an American intellectual of Lentricchia's eminence should be attracted to Merton. Merton is a man for all seasons—and reasons.

Today I was deluged with memories of my many visits to St. Joseph's Abbey in Spencer, Massachusetts. On my first trip I met Father Thomas Keating, the abbot. He'd not remember me, but I'll never forget him: tall, kind and serene, abiding in an aura of holiness. I felt it. I felt it in him and in the other monks I met. No doubt about it: Monks are God's messengers.

Every year since, I've returned to Spencer. Over twenty-five retreats. I wrote a portion of my first Merton book within its walls.

A friend of mine called and said she sometimes feels that she's talking to herself when she prays. She wonders if God is truly "there." I tried to reassure her that doubt is an intrinsic part of the inner journey and of spiritual growth.

Later, I spent the rainy afternoon reading Merton's essay, "Contemplation in a World of Action." He says that Christians must "live through this crisis of belief and grow to a more complete personal and Christian integration of experience."[62] By integration he means an integration of God's absence and presence.

Naturally one questions the how of living "through this crisis." Merton's answer is the sacraments and prayer. What other answer could there be?

Thunderstorm. At nine this morning so dark it was like night.

My return to teaching looms ahead. And then my first retreat. I am now certain about how I will approach the direction of the retreat. But how successful it will be still makes me nervous. My concern is not a selfish one. I have no desire to dazzle my audience. My hope is that during the day they will hear the saving word, the one that offers hope and inspiration, the word that serves as the impetus to know more about Merton and contemplation—to know God!

Today I received a phone call from a *Boston Globe* editor. Seems the newspaper wants to publish my essay, "Teaching and Contemplation." This is a first! I never really thought Boston's leading paper would publish something so "religious." It confirms my belief that the world is indeed very much interested in contemplation, as interested as it was when Merton arrived on the literary scene in the late 1940s.

My essay, the Prologue of this book, is really a paraphrase of what Simone Weil and Thomas Merton have often said, and they only repeated what Christ said two thousand years ago: In losing yourself you will find yourself. The simplicity of it is mind-boggling.

Commonweal's sensitive and insightful article on Pope John XXIII and his upcoming beatification sent me back to Merton's journals. He admired and loved the late pope. As do I. As a young man I devoured the pope's published journals. This morning I searched for the volume containing those journals and couldn't find it. I lent it to a friend, I suppose, as I did all books that excite me. Today I shall stop off at the Pauline bookstore to purchase the paperback. That is, if the rains of Ranchipur diminish to allow a meager visibility.

Merton's entry for June 1, 1963, the Vigil of Pentecost:

> Pope John is dying and perhaps dead. Already yesterday at this time he was in a coma, in an oxygen tent, with the papal guards around his apartments. Last night he was conscious for a moment, they say, and smiled and blessed those around him. I have been thinking of him all day and praying for him...the world owes him a great debt, in his simplicity. It is hard to feel that we can do without someone like him. He has done so much in four years...to remind people that Christian charity is not a pure fiction.[63]

In all things Merton is drawn toward simplicity and love.

Although Mott's biography remains the definitive one, Shannon's biography is an appealing one because he puts Merton in the context of his time. And this is useful. He does a fine job with the Merton and Pasternak correspondence. During his life, Merton struck up a friendship with two future Nobel Prize winners behind the Iron Curtain: Milosz and Pasternak. Merton fell in love with Pasternak's novel *Doctor Zhivago*, or rather he fell in love with the character Lara whom, he writes in a letter to P, he met in a dream. Her name was Proverb.

The Proverb dreams are prophetic; Merton meets her in his nurse a few years later.

In the midst of his love affair with M., Merton writes:

> What do I fear most? Forgetting, ignorance of the inmost truth of my being, to forget who I am, to be lost in what I am not, to fail my own inner truth, to get carried away in what is not true to me, what is outside me, what imposes itself on me from the outside. But what is this? It can take manifold forms. I must fear and distrust them all. Yet I cannot help being to some extent influenced by what is outside me, and hence I must accept that influence to some extent. But always in such a way that it increases my awareness, my remembrance, my understanding, instead of diminishing these.[64]

Merton surely knows what he must do in regard to M. And with God's grace he does what I believe is the right thing.

Dr. Padovano's *The Human Journey* offers a fine overview of Merton's life. He says Merton's mind is essentially "poetic." Merton's prose is often poetic. But his poetry is too often prosaic. Every once in a while there were remarkable marriages of prose and poetry, like the haunting prose of "Firewatch," "Rain and Rhinoceros," and the prose-poem "Hagia Sophia."

As I mentioned, Merton's was often a spirituality of reading. So is mine. All my life I have turned to the "beautiful bare text," Robert Frost's phrase, to the point that my reading became my *lectio divina*. Merton transformed his reading into sacred activity; it was a journey toward sapiential reading, toward the meaning not only of the text but of life. Along the way he culled all available wisdom to pass on to his companions: his readers. To that end his own writing became treasures of *sapientia*, or wisdom. In one of his reading notebooks, Merton writes:

> Perhaps I write to slow down my reading & reflect more. In the hermitage I read much more slowly, take more time, cover less ground. In the morning, with two & a half hours of reading, I still read very little, & the time is gone like a half hour. There is not quantitative estimate of this time. It is simply a "period of reading" with its own quality.[65]

His reading takes upon itself the quality of meditation.

Merton's reading of texts and of nature leads him into a more intense living in the Now. One does not read the moment, however. One forgets it. A different spirituality. Or is it?

Merton's essay "The Pasternak Affair" takes me back to my young adulthood when the movie *Doctor Zhivago* surpassed the fame of the novel. (Who can ever forget Julie Christie?) I wonder if anyone reads *Doctor Zhivago* any more. It's not listed on our school's reading list. (Chekhov, Tolstoy, Dostoevsky, and Solzhenitsyn are.) However, Merton was excited and intrigued by it, and wrote several letters to Pasternak, who had refused to accept the Nobel Prize for literature.

It's rather poignant to read Merton describing Pasternak as the symbol of his age: A person/artist of honesty, integrity, sincerity, personal warmth, and generosity, "a genuine human being stranded in a mad world. He immediately became a symbol, and all those who felt it was important not to be mad attached themselves in some way to him."[66]

How ironic: Padovano argues that *Merton* is the symbol of our time.

Sunday. A beautiful morning with the sun shining and the air cool. On my lawn lay a few brown leaves, precursors of autumn. It was a nice surprise to open the *Boston Globe* to find my article on teaching and contemplation. The title, however, "Teaching Students How to Lose Themselves in Thought," was deceptive. They were afraid to use the word contemplation in the title. That's okay because I understand the exigencies of publishing. I'm thankful that the editor Shirley Newsome had the courage to publish what is essentially a spiritual piece.

Spent the morning reflecting on Merton's essay, "The Power and Meaning of Love." I take away two important quotations:

> Man's greatest dignity, his most essential and peculiar power, the most intimate secret of his humanity is his capacity to love.[67]

> Love is the key to the meaning of life. It is at the same time transformation in Christ and the discovery of Christ. As we grow in love and in unity with those who are loved by Christ (that is to say, all men), we become more and more capable of apprehending and obscurely grasping something of the tremendous reality of Christ in the world, Christ in ourselves and Christ in our fellow man.[68]

How crucial it was, therefore, that Merton finally learn that he indeed was capable of love. Thus his affair with M. is an integral part of Merton's spiritual journey.

Today I e-mailed Jonathan for the whereabouts of Merton's essay "Day of a Stranger." Quick response: "Cunningham's *Thomas Merton: Spiritual Master.*" I hit my forehead in remembrance.

This essay must be read again and again. Will spend the rest of the day meditating upon it. Food for the soul!

When Merton wrote "Day of a Stranger," he was already living in his hermitage. The essay began as a response to a South American inquiry about how he spent his day. Merton simply but poetically describes his day: a whole (holy) day that "marries" the contemplative, artistic, and liturgical interests that imbued his life.

To me Merton is at his most Zen-like when he daily collects drinking water, chops his wood, washes the coffee pot with rain water, sweeps his floor, cuts his bread, and prepares a meal. He listens to birds and the wind. He watches the clouds. Even approaching the outhouse takes upon itself the quality of sacred ritual as he addresses the king snake he once discovered inside, "Are you in there, you bastard?"[69]

Milosz accused Merton of being a romantic, of seeing only nature's benign beauty and not nature "red in tooth and claw." But on his walk to the abbey, Merton passes the place where "I saw the fox run daintily and carefully for cover carrying a rabbit in his mouth."[70] He says this matter-of-factly, but it is a significant growth; he no longer averts his eyes from nature's crueler aspects.

Merton says he is never alone in his hermitage. Poets, novelists, mystics and Asian philosophers abide with him. Poets: Rilke, Zukofsky, and Edwin Muir. Novelists: Camus and O'Connor. Mystics: Teresa of Avila and Julian of Norwich. Asians: Lao Tzu and Chuang Tzu. All of these writers transform his life: "The hermit life is cool." Cool because there is no need of "here" or "there." Place is insignificant, he says. But I don't buy it. Merton needs a certain kind of place in order to "be" himself. He needs silence and solitude. He needs his books. He's not that detached.

I have returned to Merton's poetry. In his poem "The Biography" there is the opening stanza:

> The blood runs down the walls of Cambridge town
> As useless as the waters of the narrow river
> While pub and alley gamble for His vesture.[71]

The reference is to his wild, promiscuous days at Cambridge University. So wild that at one party there was a mock crucifixion. The palm of Merton's hand revealed the scar of that orgiastic night. Merton never forgot Cambridge. The paradox is that although it was the locus of his Augustinian youth, it was also the place where he read Dante for the first time. Dante was the first of the great poets who "sang" Merton into conversion.

For several years after the publication of his first book of poems and his autobiography, Merton was trapped within the persona of the ideal, saintly monk. He knew the falsehood of such a mask. I too wanted him to be a saint. I had canonized him in my own mind after reading *The Seven Storey Mountain.* But he was human and frail in so many ways. That's why I am touched by his poem "Whether There Is Enjoyment in Bitterness."

> This afternoon, let me
> Be a sad person. Am I not
> Permitted (like other men)
> To be sick of myself?[72]

What is so poignant is that the monk Merton who has taken a vow of obedience asks for permission to be a "sad person." The poem certainly dispels the notion of the happy Friar Tuck image. Monks, like us, have their good and bad days.

Merton defines contemplation over a hundred times in his writing. I consider this his best: "Contemplation is essentially a listening in silence."[73]

How many times as an educator have I said to my students, "Be quiet and pay attention"? And is that not exactly what we must do as contemplatives? Merton would concur 100 percent.

In two weeks I return to school. In less than a month I conduct my first Merton retreat. I'd not be honest if I said I wasn't nervous about both. New students: all unknown enigmas. And also my retreatants: They signed up to attend; they will want something special. A special prayer to the Holy Spirit from this day forward.

August heat and humidity have returned. I am still receiving e-mail about my essay in the *Boston Globe*. Seems it moved many people, both educators and noneducators alike. Amazing how one article in a newspaper can touch so many lives. And surprising how many people are interested in Merton's poetry. I hope I have space for all those who wish to attend this retreat. I'd expected about fifteen people, but now it's more likely twice that number.

Every Merton anthology should include his essay "Philosophy of Solitude." This essay was not intended only for religious but also for lay people like myself who spend much time in solitude.

Merton writes, "Hence the vocation to solitude is not a vocation to the warm narcissistic dream of a private religion. It is a vocation to become fully awake."[74] Here Merton is at his most Thoreauvian; Thoreau said, "To be awake is to be alive!" Merton also observes that the true solitary is marked by a "great simplicity." To truly understand the mature Merton, one must read "The Day of a Stranger," where we meet a Merton of great simplicity.

We're now in September, and summer has returned in full force: hot and humid. Compelled to turn on the air-conditioner, for my sake as well as my dog's.

My retreat day comes closer and closer. How gratifying to be still receiving inquiries, even two weeks after my essay was published. Seems it was also published in another paper, in Connecticut, according to an e-mail I received from an English graduate student who wishes to attend my retreat.

I am still preparing. Today I outlined what I intend to cover in the morning session, an overview of Merton's life and an examination of several of his mystical experiences. Some critics may disagree with what I consider "mystical." To verify the characteristics of the mystical experience, I returned to William James's *Varieties of Religious Experience*. He offers four criteria:

1. Ineffability (words fail to describe the experience)
2. Noetic quality (new states of consciousness carrying a sense of authority into the time beyond the immediate experience)
3. Transience (the experience does not last)
4. Passivity (a feeling that one is in the grasp of a superior power)[75]

After his conversion, Merton vacationed in Cuba where he experienced an extraordinary event at Mass at the Church of St. Francis in Havana. At the singing of the creed, Merton was pierced by a mystical light that, although "intangible," struck him like a "thunderclap." As previously mentioned, "It was as if I had been suddenly illuminated by being blinded by the manifestation of God's presence."[76] The experience had nothing in it of sense or imagination; it "disarmed" all metaphor and images. But it was "immediate contact" with "the Truth Who was now physically really and substantially before me on the altar."[76] In short, Merton says that God was right before him.

This experience had all the criteria as outlined by James. Merton admits that even metaphor fails to describe what he'd undergone; after the fact he is still affected by its radiance. "It left a breathless joy and a clean peace and happiness that stayed for hours and it was something I have never forgotten"; he relates that it "lasted only a moment."[78]

No doubt about it: Merton was gifted with a glimpse beyond the veil.

To help him make his decision about becoming a Trappist, Merton prayed to the Little Flower, St. Therese. "Show me the way," he implored. Just as he offered the prayer, he became almost preternaturally aware of his surroundings; he was "aware of the wood, the trees, the dark hills, the wet night wind, and then clearer than any of these obvious realities, in my imagination, I started to hear the great bell of Gethsemani."[79] The sound of the bell was what convinced him. It was tolling for Merton to come to Kentucky.

There is an *unselfing* here. Merton shifts his attention to nature's beauty and then back again to an inner landscape. He reminds himself that he's only imagining the sounding bell until he realizes that it is the very time the bell would indeed be ringing to announce the Salve Regina of Compline at Gethsemani. He seeks out Father Philotheus who tells him he sees no obstacle to Merton's becoming a priest. Then he knows what he must do?

It's one of the most dramatic scenes of his autobiography, full of excellent description and edge-of-chair suspense. And when he finally decides to become a Trappist, I for one felt joyous about his intention to "disappear into God."

Much has been written about the Louisville Vision. It's an important breakthrough because Merton's self-loathing is no longer projected onto the world. This implies that he learned to forgive himself, to accept himself, to love himself through God's grace. Thus he can joyously say, "I have the immense joy of being *man*, a member of a race in which God Himself became incarnate."

Years ago by chance I read one of the great underrated novels of the twentieth century, *The Fountain* by Charles Morgan. It concerns an English officer imprisoned during World War I. Sequestered with a solitude and silence he'd never before experienced, he is inspired to write a history of the contemplative life in the Western world. When the novel was published in 1932, it was a bestseller in England and later in America. I often wondered if Merton as a young man had read *The Fountain;* it would be the very thing he would be drawn to, this man whose spiritual way is so grounded in *Logos*.

Charles Morgan's wife, novelist Hilda Vaughn, wrote an introduction to Thomas Traherne's *Centuries,* the edition I own. I opened it today and immediately found the following passage, written in the seventeenth century:

> That you are a man should fill you with joys, and make you to overflow with praises. The privilege of your nature being infinitely infinite. And that the world serves you in this fathomless manner, exhibiting the Deity, and ministering to your blessedness, ought daily to transport you with a blessed vision, into ravishments and ecstasies.[80]

With his Louisville Vision echoing Traherne, Merton is in good company!

For anyone who takes the time to offer his attention to the Louisville Vision, he will understand how tremendously Merton grew both spiritually and psychologically. He admits to his *contemptus mundi* and to following the illusion of a "separation from the world." Yes, no doubt about it, with the Louisville Vision, Merton rejoins the family of men and women and children.

Children. Merton fathered a child he never saw. At the end of his life, he uses the metaphor of the child and the child's vision to represent all that is good in the spiritual pursuit. In fact, his whole spiritual agenda is based on retrieving paradise, open, as Christ said, only to the childlike.

A picture drawn by a four year old inspired Merton's poem "Grace's House." The beauty and simplicity of this poem are ones I hope the retreatants will enjoy. Grace's house cannot be approached by any path.

> There is no path to the summit
> No path drawn
> To Grace's house.[81]

If Grace's house symbolizes paradise ("O paradise, O child's world!"), as Merton suggests, then he is stating unequivocally that each person must find his or her own way. All there is is an arrow that points toward Grace's house.

Again, Merton left us no spiritual system like that of Ignatius or John of the Cross or Teresa of Avila; or in this century like that of Simone Weil. His work does, however, serve as an arrow that is always aimed at Christ—our True Self.

Today Pope John XXIII was beatified.

Of the twelve poems I'll address during the retreat, I consider "Night-Flowering Cactus" the most difficult. For my retreatants to understand it I must speak about the *via negativa*, or what is commonly called apophatic (wordless) mysticism. Merton's mysticism was definitely along the dark path, beautifully captured in this poem, which becomes accessible when one accepts the image of a flower delivering a soliloquy. Listening to the poem becomes our prayer.

The number of people enrolled in the Merton retreat has tripled—all because of my essay in the *Globe*. I am still in a state of amazement at the number of professors, artists, heads of English departments, and students who e-mailed me about the essay. Nothing I have ever written has elicited such a positive response.

Less than three weeks till my retreat.

"Love Winter When the Plant Says Nothing" is not an easy poem either. It too illustrates the *via negativa*. It reminds me of Wallace Stevens's "The Snowman." But it's not as cold as Stevens's poem: Merton's poem is warmed by love. When should we love? Always. Even when there is no answer, no consolations, no sun, the "golden zero." Love without ceasing.

Closer. Two weeks from today I conduct my retreat. I have prepared a package in the form of a folder containing: copies of twelve poems by Merton, copies of four of Merton's radiant (mystical) experiences, a section of the short story "The Bear" by William Faulkner, my own essay from the *Globe*, and poems I think they'd like: Herbert's "Love Bade Me Welcome" and Hazo's "The Holy Surprise of Right Now."

Merton was overwhelmed by Faulkner's short story, and I plan to play the tape during which he explains its mystical symbolism. It's a half hour long, but I believe it's important enough to take the time.

I am almost certain some retreatants will ask, "What is Merton's method of prayer?" I am prepared with a statement from one of Merton's letters—actually two—in which he suggests what people can do.

> I heartily recommend, as a form of prayer, the Russian and Greek business where you get off somewhere quiet...breathe deeply and rhythmically with the diaphragm, holding your breath for a bit each time and letting it out easily: and while holding it, saying "in your heart" (aware of the place of your heart, as if the words were spoken in the very center of your being with all the sincerity you can muster): "Lord Jesus Christ Son of God have mercy on me a sinner." Just keep saying this for a while, of course, with simple faith, and the awareness of the indwelling, etc. It is a simple form of prayer, and fundamental, and the breathing part makes it easier to keep your mind on what you are doing. That's about it as far as I go with methods. After that, pray as the Spirit moves you....[82]

He later writes, "I like the rosary too. Because, though I am not very articulate about Mary, I am pretty much wound up in Our Lady, and have some Russian ideas about her too: that she is the most perfect expression of the mystery of the Wisdom of God."[83]

Retreat Day:
September 23, 2000

I didn't sleep much last night. Just hope everything goes well today. I look out the window: promises to be sunny, but I know from watching the weather channel that the clouds will roll in around noon. But I don't care. It isn't the weather that will make this day a success or failure.

I drove to Forest Hills Station to pick up my friend Jack who offered to help me with the morning registration. We parked near the entrance and carried in all the materials I'd loaded in the car: my tape and CD player, my box with hand-outs and the Merton books I'd have to read from, and a carton of my own books in case anyone would want to purchase them. And finally I carried in my precious icon of Christ enfolded in a towel. I unwrapped it for Pam, the receptionist with whom I'd been dealing all along, and set up the icon on an easel. She was overwhelmed by its beauty, and I was glad, for that's just the reaction I hoped for.

Registration began with a man who said he sent a check for which I had no record. We let him in on faith! The rest of the registration went smoothly. It was nice to put a face to all the e-mail messages I received about my *Globe* article. At 9:30 sharp I began the retreat by reading aloud Merton's famous prayer that begins, "My Lord God, I have no idea where I am going. I do not see the road ahead of me...." I joked that Merton's prayer was most appropriate because I too didn't know the road ahead of me in this, my first Merton retreat. They were open and receptive and laughed, and that rendered me brave enough to proceed.

I just took off by referring everyone to the *Globe* article, and then I talked about Simone Weil at length and illustrated the connection between her and Merton. Thus the morning flew by with my addressing the importance of attention in Merton's life. The retreatants were intrigued with the five moments of radiant attention I employed as a framework of Merton's life. We closely read these excerpts that I had copied for them.

The afternoon session we devoted to a tape of Merton's teaching Faulkner to the novices, and later we read his poetry. Of the two sessions the morning was the better. The afternoon tape after lunch was too long (half an hour) and Merton's voice wasn't clear enough for everyone to hear. I'll not use the tape again.

All in all it was a moving experience. I could tell everyone enjoyed themselves. At the breaks I even sold a few books!

Aftermath:
Reflections on the Retreat

Although I ended the retreat at 4:00 P.M., I remained for an hour more speaking with retreatants who just couldn't get enough of Thomas Merton. A man in his thirties kept shaking my hand, saying over and over that he'd been "looking for something" for so many years, and he'd felt he'd found it in Merton. Because he was a bit vague about this "something," I asked him what in particular about Merton appealed to him. "That someone so flawed could still live a holy life." When he said this, I noticed (and was moved by) the tears in his eyes. Merton had spoken to this young man who departed with a greater desire to know more about Merton; I suspect he too was a flawed person but aflame with a deep love of God.

Merton's humanness was the theme of most of the comments made to me during the post-retreat dialogue. Again and again retreatants observed that Thomas Merton was so very human and accessible. One said, "We don't need another plaster saint." Another remark that impressed me came from a woman in her eighties. Diminutive and with eyes alight with intelligence, she looked up at me and said, "Thank you for reading Merton's description of his prayer. I'm not that good at prayer, but I say the Jesus Prayer all the time." I tried to assure her that she was likely a deep contemplative and didn't know it. She laughed when I said this, but when she saw that I was serious, she said, "Me a contemplative? Why, I never thought about that." And she left with a wistful look in her eyes.

A grade school teacher shared with me that she had been a fan of Merton all her adult life. Although she had read and been nourished by all his major spiritual classics, she'd never read any of his poetry. I smiled and encouraged her to read Merton's *Selected Poetry*, a selection made by the poet himself. I have to admit that her remark pleased me the most because my retreat was intended to introduce people to Merton's poetry, the portion of his opus, I still feel, that is undervalued.

Finally, there was no one in the room except me and my friend Jack. Jack had mingled with the retreatants all day; he was my source of information about how the retreat was going over. When I expressed doubt about the success of the retreat—I was particularly upset by the poor quality of the Merton tape—he quickly allayed my fears. "People were fascinated with Merton's mystical experiences," he said, "In fact, I heard several say that they wanted to know more about them." He also said he'd heard people discussing Merton's love affair with M., and his fascination with Buddhism.

When I prepared my retreat talk, I had some reservations about addressing Merton's intimate relationship with his nurse. Over the years, I had heard many negative remarks about Merton, some even dismissing him as a spiritual writer because of this affair. But I decided that Merton is what he is. He would be the first one to say he wasn't perfect. Therefore I gave the facts about his love affair, knowing it might be a gamble because it could turn some people off.

Although Merton had the affair, he finally came to his senses and broke it off; he knew what was right and acted accordingly. Jack informed me that one woman dismissed the whole thing as "male menopause." I smiled, an explanation I had never thought of.

The other issue was Merton's interest in Buddhism. When I mentioned this in my presentation, a retreatant asked me why Merton's seemingly most mystical experience happened before a representation of Buddha and not Christ. I replied that an epiphany can happen anywhere God wants it to happen. It could have happened on a street in San Francisco, in a small chapel in Alaska, or in his hotel room. God graced Merton with an overwhelming illumination; he perceived his life and life in general with eyes newly opened by the beauty of the stone Buddhas of Polonnaruwa.

There was also some concern among retreatants about the rumors of Merton's leaving his abbey and his Catholic religion to become a Buddhist. Such talk is gossip. Merton was a Trappist monk and a Catholic priest through and through; he greatly loved his fellow monks of Gethsemani and missed them very much while he was on his journey to the East. He was completely dedicated to his contemplative vocation. Whether or not he would have left Gethsemani to establish a new foundation or hermitage elsewhere is mere speculation.

I drove Jack to his apartment in Boston. As he was stepping out of the car, he said, "Stop worrying, it was a great retreat...we all loved it."

Driving back to my own home, I was thinking of my next retreat: a weekend retreat also at St. Stephen Priory. Two full days! And I hoped I would have enough people enrolled to run it....

Endnotes

1. This chapter is adapted from an article that originally appeared in the *Boston Globe* August 20, 2000. Its description of the importance of a contemplative attentiveness not only in teaching but also in the spiritual life makes evident the influence of Merton's life and writings upon my own thinking.

2. Ernest Hemingway, *The Short Stories* (New York: Collier Books, 1986), pp. 209–10.

3. George Steiner, *Errata: An Examined Life* (New Haven: Yale University Press, 1999), p. 27.

4. Francis Thompson, *Poems of Francis Thompson* (New York: Century, 1932), p. 77.

5. Robert Lax, *Love Had a Compass: Journals and Poetry* (New York: Grove Press, 1996), p. 55.

6. Ibid., p. 210.

7. Thomas Merton, *Thoughts in Solitude* (New York: Farrar, Straus, Giroux, 1956), p. 83.

8. Thomas Merton, *The Collected Poems of Thomas Merton* (New York: New Directions, 1977), p. 212.

9. Rob Baker and Gray Henry, eds., *Merton and Sufism* (Louisville: Fons Vitae, 1999), p. 217.

10. Thomas Merton, *Hidden Ground of Love, Letters*, ed. William Shannon (New York: Farrar, Straus, Giroux, 1985). pp. 472–73.

11. Thomas Merton, *Conjectures of a Guilty Bystander* (New York: Doubleday, 1966), p. 270.

12. Merton, *Hidden Ground of Love*, pp. 63–64.

13. Thomas Merton, *New Seeds of Contemplation* (New York: New Directions, 1961), p. 1.

14. Pope John Paul II, *Letter to Artists* (Boston: Pauline Books & Media, 1999), p. 32.

15. Robert Fagin, *Striving Towards Being: The Letters of Thomas Merton and Czeslaw Milosz* (New York: Farrar, Straus, Giroux, 1997), p. 150.

16. Ibid., p. 82.

17. Merton, *Collected Poems*, p. 35.

18. Thomas Merton, *The Intimate Merton: His Life from His Journals*, ed. Patrick Hart and Jonathan Montaldo (San Francisco: HarperSanFrancisco, 1999), p. 129.

19. T. S. Eliot, *Murder in the Cathedral* (New York: Harcourt, Brace, 1935), p. 70.

20. Gerard Manley Hopkins, *The Poems of Gerard Manley Hopkins*, ed. W. H. Gardner and N. H. Mackenzie (London: Oxford University Press, 1967), p. 31.

21. Merton, *Thoughts in Solitude*, p. 62.

22. Thomas Merton, *Eighteen Poems* (New York: New Directions, 1985), third poem in a volume not paginated.

23. Ibid., last page of text.

24. Thomas Merton, *The Literary Essays of Thomas Merton* (New York: New Directions, 1985), p. 339.

25. Steiner, *Errata*, p. 27.

26. Emily Dickinson, *The Complete Poems of Emily Dickinson*, ed. Thomas Johnson (Boston: Little, Brown, 1960), p. 1212.

27. Thomas Merton, *Honorable Reader: Reflections on My Work* (New York: Crossroad, 1981), "Appendix 2 Thomas Merton's Graph Evaluating His Own Books 1967."

28. Merton, *Collected Poems*, p. 90.

29. Ibid., p. 96.

30. Ibid., p. 279.

31. Samuel Hazo, *The Holy Surprise of Right Now* (Fayetteville, Ark.: University of Arkansas Press, 1996), p. 258.

32. Thomas Merton, *Raids on the Unspeakable* (New York: New Directions, 1964), p. 23.

33. Blurb by Kenneth Woodward of *Newsweek* from the back cover of *The Intimate Merton*.

34. Merton, *The Intimate Merton*, p. 293.

35. Ibid., p. 302.

36. Thomas Merton, *A Vow of Conversation* (New York: Farrar, Straus, Giroux, 1988).

37. Alan Watts, *In My Own Way: An Autobiography* (New York: Vintage Books, 1973), p. 444.

38. Merton, *Collected Poems*, p. 315.

39. Ibid., p. 239.

40. Merton, *New Seeds of Contemplation*, p. 21.

41. Ibid., p. 227.

42. Thomas Merton, *No Man Is an Island* (New York: Harcourt, Brace, 1955), p. 194.

43. Merton, *Honorable Reader*, p. 67.

44. Henri Nouwen, *Spiritual Journals* (New York: Continuum, 1998), p. 71.

45. Henri Nouwen, *Sabbatical Journey: The Diary of His Final Year* (New York: Crossroad, 1998), p. 5.

46. Merton, *New Seeds of Contemplation*, p. 221.

47. Ibid., p. 78.

48. Thomas Merton, *The Way of Chuang Tzu* (New York: New Directions, 1969), p. 10.

49. Ibid., p. 31.

50. Merton, *Literary Essays*, p. 276.

51. Merton, *Conjectures of a Guilty Bystander*, p. 69.

52. Brother Patrick Hart and Jonathan Montaldo, in their introduction to Merton, *The Intimate Merton*, p. xi.

53. Ibid., p. xiii.

54. Thomas Merton, *The New Man* (New York: Farrar, Straus, Giroux, 1961), p. 170.

55. Thomas Merton, *The Road to Joy: Letters to New and Old Friends*, ed. Robert Daggy (New York: Farrar, Straus, Giroux, 1989), p. 141.

56. Ibid., p. 156.

57. Thomas Merton, *The Seven Storey Mountain* (New York: Harcourt, Brace, 1948), p. 274.

58. Dennis D. Cooper, ed., *Thomas Merton and James Laughlin: Selected Letters* (New York: W. W. Norton, 1997), p. 378.

59. Lawrence S. Cunningham, ed., *Thomas Merton: Spiritual Master, The Essential Writings* (New York: Paulist Press, 1992), p. 424.

60. Frank Lentricchia, *The Edge of Night: A Confession* (New York: Random House, 1994), p. 47.

61. Ibid., p. 46.

62. Merton, *Spiritual Master*, p. 374.

63. Merton, *The Intimate Merton*, p. 208.

64. Ibid., p. 296.

65. Claire Hoertz Badaracco, "Cultural Resistance and Literary Identity: Merton's Reading Notebooks," *Merton Annual*, volume 10, p. 198.

66. Thomas Merton, *Disputed Questions* (New York: Harcourt, Brace, 1985), p. 98.

67. Merton, *Disputed Questions*, p. 123.

68. Ibid.

69. Merton, *Spiritual Master*, p. 220.

70. Ibid.

71. Merton, *Collected Poems*, p. 104.

72. Ibid., p. 231.

73. Thomas Merton, *Contemplative Prayer* (New York: Doubleday, 1966), p. 90.

74. Merton, *Disputed Questions*, p. 184.

75. William James, *Varieties of Religious Experience* (New York: Random House, 1902), pp. 371–72.

76. Merton, *The Seven Storey Mountain*, p. 284.

77. Ibid., p. 285.

78. Ibid.

79. Ibid., p. 364.

80. Thomas Trahern, *Centuries* (London: Faith Press, 1960), p. 68.

81. Merton, *Collected Poems*, p. 330.

82. Merton, *Hidden Ground of Love*, p. 392.

83. Ibid.

Bibliography

Baker, Rob, and Gray Henry, eds. *Merton and Sufism*. Louisville: Fons Vitae, 1999.

Dickinson, Emily. *The Complete Poems of Emily Dickinson*. Edited by Thomas Johnson. Boston: Little, Brown, 1960.

Eliot, T. S. *Murder in the Cathedral*. New York: Harcourt, Brace, 1935.

Furlong, Monica. *Zen Effects: The Life of Alan Watts*. Boston: Houghton Mifflin, 1986.

Hazo, Samuel. *The Holy Surprise of Right Now*. Fayetteville, Ark.: University of Arkansas Press, 1996.

Hemingway, Ernest. *The Short Stories*. New York: Collier Books, 1986.

Hopkins, Gerard Manley. *The Poems of Gerard Manley Hopkins*. Edited by W. H. Gardner and N. H. Mackenzie. London: Oxford University Press, 1967.

James, William. *Varieties of Religious Experience*. New York: Random House, 1902.

John Paul II. *Letter to Artists*. Boston: Pauline Books and Media, 1999.

Lax, Robert. *Love Had a Compass: Journals and Poetry*. New York: Grove Press, 1996.

Lentricchia, Frank. *The Edge of Night: A Confession*. New York: Random House 1994.

Merton, Thomas. *The Collected Poems of Thomas Merton*. New York: New Directions, 1977.

Merton, Thomas. *Conjectures of a Guilty Bystander*. New York: Doubleday, 1966.

Merton, Thomas. *The Courage for Truth: Letters to Writers*. Edited by Christine M. Bochen. New York: Farrar, Straus, Giroux, 1993.

Merton, Thomas. *Dancing in the Water of Life, Journals: Volume Five 1963–1965*. Edited by Robert E. Daggy. San Francisco: HarperSanFrancisco, 1997.

Merton, Thomas. *Disputed Questions*. New York: Harcourt, Brace, 1985.

Merton, Thomas. *Eighteen Poems*. New York: New Directions, 1985.

Merton, Thomas. *Entering the Silence, Journals: Volume Two 1941–1952*. Edited by Jonathan Montaldo. San Francisco: HarperSanFrancisco, 1996.

Merton, Thomas. *The Geography of Lograire.* New York: New Directions, 1968.

Merton, Thomas. *The Hidden Ground of Love.* New York: Farrar, Straus, Giroux, 1985.

Merton, Thomas. *The Intimate Merton: His Life from His Journals.* Edited by Patrick Hart and Jonathan Montaldo. San Francisco: HarperSanFrancisco, 1999.

Merton, Thomas. *Learning to Love, Journals: Volume Six 1966–1967.* Edited by Christine M. Bochen. San Francisco: HarperSanFrancisco, 1997.

Merton, Thomas. *The Literary Essays of Thomas Merton.* Edited by Patrick Hart. New York: New Directions, 1981.

Merton, Thomas. *The New Man.* New York: Farrar, Straus, Giroux, 1961.

Merton, Thomas. *New Seeds of Contemplation.* New York: New Directions, 1961.

Merton, Thomas. *No Man Is an Island.* New York: Doubleday, 1955.

Merton, Thomas. *The Other Side of the Mountain, Journals: Volume Seven 1967–1968.* Edited by Patrick Hart. San Francisco: HarperSanFrancisco, 1999.

Merton, Thomas. *Raids on the Unspeakable.* New York: New Directions, 1964.

Merton, Thomas. *The Road to Joy: Letters to New and Old* Friends. Edited by Robert Daggy. New York: Farrar, Straus, Giroux, 1989.

Merton, Thomas. *Run to the Mountain, Journals: Volume One 1939–1941.* Edited by Patrick Hart. San Francisco: HarperSanFrancisco, 1995.

Merton, Thomas. *A Search for Solitude, Journals: Volume Three 1952–1960.* Edited by Lawrence S. Cunningham. San Francisco: HarperSanFrancisco, 1996.

Merton, Thomas. *The Seven Storey Mountain.* New York: Harcourt, Brace, 1948.

Merton, Thomas. *Thomas Merton: Spiritual Master, The Essential Writings.* Edited by Lawrence S. Cunningham. New York: Paulist Press, 1992.

Merton, Thomas. *Thoughts in Solitude.* New York: Farrar, Straus, Giroux, 1956.

Merton, Thomas. *Turning Towards the World, Journals: Volume Four 1960–1963.* Edited by Victor A. Kramer. San Francisco: HarperSanFrancisco, 1996.

Merton, Thomas. *A Vow of Conversation.* New York: Farrar, Straus, Giroux, 1988.

Merton, Thomas. *The Way of Chuang Tzu.* New York: New Directions, 1969.

Merton, Thomas. *What Is Contemplation?* Springfield, Ill.: Templegate Publishers, 1981.

Merton, Thomas, and Czelaw Milosz. *Striving Towards Being: The Letters of Thomas Merton and Czelaw Milosz.* Edited by Robert Fagin. New York: Farrar, Straus, Giroux, 1997.

Merton, Thomas, and James Laughlin. *Thomas Merton and James Laughlin: Selected Letters.* Edited by Dennis D. Cooper. New York: W. W. Norton, 1997.

Nouwen, Henri. *Sabbatical Journey: The Diary of His Final Year.* New York: Crossroad, 1998.

Nouwen, Henri. *Spiritual Journals.* New York: Continuum, 1998.

Steiner, George. *Errata: An Examined Life.* New Haven: Yale University Press, 1999.

Traherne, Thomas. *Centuries.* London: Faith Press, 1960.